REA's interactive flashcards™

USMLE
STEP 1
U.S. Medical Licensing Examination

**Staff of Research and Education Association,
Dr. M. Fogiel, Director**

Research & Education Association
61 Ethel Road West
Piscataway, New Jersey 08854

REA's INTERACTIVE FLASHCARDS™ USMLE STEP 1

Printed in the United States of America

Library of Congress Catalog Card Number 98-66566

International Standard Book Number 0-87891-167-7

Research & Education Association, Piscataway, New Jersey 08854

REA's Interactive Flashcards
What they're for
How to use them

They come in a book, not in a box of hundreds of loose cards.

They are most useful as test time approaches to help you check your test readiness.

They are a good tool for self-study and also for group study. They can even be used as a competitive game to see who scores best.

They work with any text.

The interactive feature is a unique learning tool. With it, you can write in your own answer to each question which you can then check against the correct answer provided on the flip side of each card.

You will find that the flashcards in a book have several advantages over flashcards in a box.

You don't have to cope with hundreds of loose cards. Whenever you want to study, you don't have to decide beforehand which cards you are likely to need; you don't have to pull them out of a box (and later return them in their proper place). You can just open the book and get going without ado.

A very detailed index will guide you to whatever topics you want to cover.

A number of blank card pages is included, in case you want to construct some of your own Q's and A's.

You can take along REA's Flashcard book anywhere, ready for use when you are. You don't need to tote along the box or a bunch of loose cards.

REA's Flashcard books have been carefully put together with REA's customary concern for quality. We believe you will find them an excellent review and study tool.

Dr. M. Fogiel
Program Director

P.S. As you could tell, you could see all the flashcards in the book while you were in the store; they aren't sealed in shrink-wrap.

Questions

What is the most common cause of contact dermatitis in the United States?

*Your Own Answer*_____

A tumor in the pelvis of a 40-year-old woman has caused an obstruction of the umbilical arteries, resulting in a compromised blood flow to what structure?

*Your Own Answer*_____

If the parathyroid glands are inadvertently removed during thyroidectomy, what will happen?

*Your Own Answer*_____

Correct Answers

A1

Four-fifths of contact dermatitis cases are caused by universal irritants such as soaps, detergents, and organic solvents.

A2

Since the superior vesicle arteries are usually branches of the umbilical arteries, a portion of the urinary bladder would be ischemic in this case, even though the inferior vesicle arteries, from the internal iliac artery, would not be occluded.

A3

The removal of the parathyroid glands would result in a fatal drop in blood calcium levels, leading to tetany (spastic contraction of skeletal muscle) and the death of the patient.

Questions

Q4

A 78-year-old female presents with inability to control her urine flow. She was diagnosed with mixed incontinence by her physician. What therapies can assist her in regaining control of her bladder?

*Your Own Answer*_____

Q5

Your patient has an extensive intra-abdominal infection, and fluid (ascites) is starting to accumulate in the peritoneal cavity. In the recumbent position, where will most of the fluid tend to accumulate?

*Your Own Answer*_____

Q6

In testicular cancer, the lymphogenous spread of tumor cells would go directly to which lymph nodes?

*Your Own Answer*_____

Correct Answers

A4

Anticholinergic agents, such as oxybutynin and propantheline, can help patients with urge incontinence by relaxing sphincter muscles. Bladder training requires the patient to resist or inhibit the sensation of urgency, to postpone voiding, and to urinate according to a timetable rather than according to urge.

A5

In the recumbent position, the hepatorenal recess is the most dependent region of the peritoneal cavity, meaning that fluid will gravitate to it.

A6

The testicular lymphatics drain to the lumbar and preaortic nodes.

Questions

Q7

When performing a thyroidectomy, why is it important to leave the posterior portion of the gland, along with its blood supply, in place?

*Your Own Answer*_____

Q8

What is the most common bacteria found in the colon?

*Your Own Answer*_____

Q9

Vitamin D deficiency is associated with which disease?

*Your Own Answer*_____

Correct Answers

A7

The parathyroid glands, embedded in the posterior part of the thyroid gland, are vital to life. Without parathyroid glands, blood calcium levels would drop to fatal levels. Thus, a portion of the thyroid gland is typically left intact, if possible.

A8

Bacteroides species is the most common bacteria in the colon. It is an obligate anaerobe.

A9

Rickets, characterized by abnormal bone development, is caused by vitamin D deficiency.

Questions

Q10

You have a patient with a tumor affecting the dorsal roots of spinal nerves S1 and S2. Where would you expect to find abnormal cutaneous sensations?

*Your Own Answer*_____

Q11

What are common side effects of furosemide?

*Your Own Answer*_____

Q12

A 51-year-old black male with a history of diabetes and renal failure presents with a painless, soft tissue mass on his right shoulder. His phosphate level was elevated. Biopsy of the mass revealed fibroblasts and collagen fibers. X-rays of the right shoulder revealed calcification of the soft tissue mass. What is the most likely diagnosis?

*Your Own Answer*_____

Correct Answers

A10

A compression of the S1 and S2 dorsal roots would result in abnormal cutaneous sensations (paraesthesiae) along the S1 and S2 dermatomes, located along the posterior aspect of the thigh, leg, and gluteal region.

A11

Furosemide inhibits electrolyte reabsorption in the distal portion of the ascending loop of Henle, which produces a diuresis. In the process, potassium and acid are not reabsorbed, producing hypokalemia and a metabolic alkalosis. Ototoxicity and hyperuricemia are additional effects of furosemide.

A12

Tumoral calcinosis is a periarticular soft tissue mass surrounded by a connective-tissue capsule and containing chalky material. This disorder is associated with diabetes, renal failure, and hyperparathyroidism. It is more prevalent in the African-American population.

Questions

Q13

What type of increase shifts the oxygen-hemoglobin dissociation curve to the left?

*Your Own Answer*_____

Q14

In a population at equilibrium, three genotypes are present in the following proportions: A/A 0.81, *a*/*a* 0.01, where A and *a* are two alleles of a certain gene. What is the frequency of allele A in the population?

*Your Own Answer*_____

Q15

Which muscle groups are most commonly affected in dermatomyositis?

*Your Own Answer*_____

Correct Answers

A13

Increased pH shifts the oxygen-hemoglobin dissocation curve to the left (thereby increasing the binding affinity of hemoglobin for oxygen). Increased CO_2, 2,3-DPG, and temperature all cause a right shift, making it easier for O_2 to dissociate at a given O_2 partial pressure.

A14

For an equilibrium population with two alleles A and a, the genotype frequencies are given by the Hardy-Weinberg Law: $(A + a)^2 = A^2 + 2Aa + a^2 = 1$ where A^2 is the frequency of the A/A homozygote, $2Aa$ is the frequency of the A/a heterozygote, and a^2 is the frequency of the a/a homozygote. Therefore, $A^2 = 0.81$, so $A = 0.9$.

A15

The most common muscles involved in dermatomyositis are the proximal muscles.

Questions

Q16

What is the function of the blood-thymus barrier?

*Your Own Answer*_____

_____

Q17

What is a thickening of the fascia lata that serves as the distal attachment for the gluteus maximus and tensor fascia latae muscles?

*Your Own Answer*_____

_____

Q18

The pudendal canal (Alcock's canal), containing the internal pudendal vessels, pudendal nerve, and dorsal nerve of the penis (clitoris), lies on the medial surface of which muscle?

*Your Own Answer*_____

_____

Correct Answers

A16

The blood-thymus barrier provides an antigen-free microenvironment for the normal development of T-cells.

A17

The iliotibial tract serves as the distal attachment for these muscles.

A18

The pudendal canal is within the deep fascia along the inner surface of the obturator internus muscle.

Questions

Q19

What is the most common dermatologic manifestation of Chédiak-Higashi syndrome?

*Your Own Answer*_____

Q20

A patient with hepatic centrilobular necrosis and fatty change of the liver might have been exposed to what substance?

*Your Own Answer*_____

Q21

Lymphocytes, plasma cells, macrophages and tissue destruction are characteristic of what type of inflammation?

*Your Own Answer*_____

Correct Answers

A19

Chédiak-Higashi is a multisystem autosomal recessive disease. Patients have central nervous system abnormalities as well as increased incidence of malignancies. They have immunologic abnormalities, such as abnormal neutrophil chemotaxis and decreased natural killer cell activity. The most common cutaneous manifestation is partial albinism. Café au lait macules and axillary freckling are common in neurofibromatosis.

A20

Carbon tetrachloride exposure leads to hepatic centrilobular necrosis and fatty change.

A21

Chronic inflammation is associated with the presence of lymphocytes, plasma cells, macrophages, attempts at repair by connective-tissue replacement, and tissue destruction. Acute inflammation is characterized by vascular changes, edema, and the transmigration of leukocytes, mostly neutrophils.

Questions

Q22

Gram-positive cocci in clumps is a typical formation for which microorganism?

*Your Own Answer*_____

Q23

The pituitary gland lies in the pituitary fossa, which is part of which structure?

*Your Own Answer*_____

Q24

What disease is associated with a replication error phenotype (i.e., RER+)?

*Your Own Answer*_____

Correct Answers

A22

Staphylococcus ssp

A23

The pituitary (hypophyseal) fossa forms a portion of the sella turcica, a part of the body of the sphenoid bone.

A24

Hereditary nonpolyposis colon cancer is a defect in DNA mismatch excision repair. It is associated with a replication error phenotype (RER+), which is noted early in the progression of colonic tumors, and manifests as a genetic instability of simple repeated sequences.

Questions

Q25

When viewing a biopsy slide of the pyloro-duode-nal junction, you notice a pathological lesion involving glands in the submucosal region of the specimen. Assuming that the specimen represents an adequate sample, what can be inferred about this particular lesion?

*Your Own Answer*_____

Q26

Lactrodectus mactans is the Latin name for what organism?

*Your Own Answer*_____

Q27

A meningioma within the interpeduncular fossa would likely result in what sign?

*Your Own Answer*_____

Correct Answers

A25

The fact that the lesion involves glands in the submucosa indicates that the lesion involves the duodenum, specifically the submucosal glands of Brunner.

A26

The black widow is also known as latrodecla. It is sometimes called hour-glass because of the red hour-glass marking on the underside of its abdomen. The rest of the body is shiny black.

A27

The oculomotor (CN III) traverses the interpeduncular fossa and would be vulnerable to a tumor or lesion in this area. Ptosis, as well as a loss of the pupillary light reflex and certain eye movements, would result from denervation of the levator palpebrae superior muscle, supplied by CN III.

Questions

Q28

A 50-year-old female presents with hot flashes, urogenital atrophy, and depression. Her gynecologist states that she is undergoing menopausal changes. What happens to sex hormone levels during menopause?

*Your Own Answer*_____

Q29

In cancer of the tip of the tongue, metastasis would initially spread to the which nodes?

*Your Own Answer*_____

Q30

Reiter's syndrome includes what symptoms?

*Your Own Answer*_____

Correct Answers

A28

Progesterone levels are nearly unmeasurable in menopause. An increase in follicle-stimulating hormone and luteinizing hormone occur as progesterone and estrogen levels dwindle, due to the loss of the negative feedback system. The relative ratio of testosterone to estradiol increases secondary to loss of estrogen levels.

A29

The submental nodes receive lymphatic drainage from the tip of the tongue.

A30

Reiter's syndrome includes nongonococcal urethritis, conjunctivitis, and arthritis. It also can present with ankylosing spondylitis and psoriasis, as well as keratoderma blennorrhagia, which is usually erythematous vericular or macular lesions on the palms and soles with hyperkeratosis. It typically presents post-venereal or intestinal infection.

Questions

Q31

Examination of cerebral neurons from patients with Alzheimer's disease demonstrate what feature?

*Your Own Answer*_____

Q32

During thyroid surgery, the parathyroid glands were inadvertently removed. What would cause a fatal drop in blood calcium levels?

*Your Own Answer*_____

Q33

Inguinal hernia in newborns, which is much more common in males, results from persistence of which structure?

*Your Own Answer*_____

Correct Answers

A31

Nerve cells from patients with Alzheimer's disease demonstrate neurofibrillary tangles. Neurofibrillary tangles are twisted clusters of fibers found inside nerve cells. Alzheimer's disease is characterized by atrophy, so one would not expect to see dendritic hypertrophy or axonal hyperplasia.

A32

The osteoclasts (under the influence of parathyroid hormone) function in maintaining blood calcium levels. Their inactivity would cause these levels to drop.

A33

In indirect inguinal hernia, the processus vaginalis fails to close. Intestinal loops may herniate through it into the scrotum or labia majoris.

Questions

Q34

In terms of radiosensitivity, is the developing CNS more or less sensitive than the adult CNS?

*Your Own Answer*_____

Q35

What are three organisms from the herpes virus group?

*Your Own Answer*_____

Q36

A six-month-old male bottlefed infant presents with persistent bronchitis that started at approximately 6 months of age. Lab studies demonstrate abnormally low levels of immunoglobulin with low B-cell counts, but normal cellular immunity. What is the most likely diagnosis?

*Your Own Answer*_____

Correct Answers

A34

The developing CNS is radiosensitive, whereas the adult CNS is radioresistant.

A35

Herpes virus is a DNA virus. It is an enveloped virus and contains herpes simplex type I, herpes simplex Type II, varicella zoster, cytomegalovirus, and Epstein-Barr virus.

A36

Low immunoglobulin levels and low B cell counts are typical of X-linked agammaglobulinemia.

Questions

Q37

A 25-year-old female presents with altered mental status and spider angiomas on exam. She was found to have cirrhosis of the liver of unknown etiology. She was not an alcoholic, and she did not take drugs. What is the most likely diagnosis?

*Your Own Answer*_____

Q38

Hirschprung's disease is caused by a lack of innervation of which part of the bowel?

*Your Own Answer*_____

Q39

What cell types are the most resistant to ionizing radiation in an adult?

*Your Own Answer*_____

Correct Answers

A37

Wilson's disease is an autosomal recessive disorder that causes accumulation of copper in the liver, brain, and other organs. Clinical signs first appear anywhere between the ages of 2 and 50, and most frequently during adolescence. Accumulation of copper in the liver often progresses to cirrhosis. Accumulation in the brain often leads to motor disturbances.

A38

Hirschprung's disease is caused by lack of ganglion cells in the bowel wall and is always restricted to the colon. It most commonly occurs in the rectosigmoid region. Newborns present with no stools and can develop megacolon proximal to the aganglionic region.

A39

Ionizing radiation tends to affect rapidly dividing cells most severely. Since central nervous system cells do not divide in adults, they are among the most resistant.

Questions

Q40

On examination, a patient with acute and massive renal failure has pronounced edema from head to foot. What is the term for this type of edema?

*Your Own Answer*_____

Q41

Are Streptococcus, Listeria, Actinomyces, and *Clostridium* examples of Gram-positive or Gram-negative bacteria?

*Your Own Answer*_____

Q42

A 54-year-old homemaker complains of headaches and palpitations. Physical examination reveals mild hypertension. MRI tests demonstrates an incidental adrenal mass. The laboratory analysis indicates increased levels of plasma norepinephrine and epinephrine as well as increased levels of urinary catecholamines. What is the most likely cell type of the tumor mass?

*Your Own Answer*_____

Correct Answers

A40

Anasarca is massive edema.

A41

All of the bacteria listed are members of the Gram-positive bacteria. Streptococcus is Gram-positive coccus; Listeria is a non-filamentous non-spore-forming Gram-positive rod; Actinomyces is a filamentous non-spore-forming Gram-positive rod; and Clostridium is an obligate anaerobic spore-forming Gram-positive rod.

A42

Chromaffin cell is the most likely cell type. On the basis of the clinical findings, the biochemical laboratory results, and the anatomic localization, this patient most likely has a pheochromocytoma. Although this uncommon cancer can arise anywhere in the sympathetic ganglia, it is often localized to the chromaffin cells of the adrenal gland.

Questions

Q43

Since 1930, which form of cancer has become the most fatal?

*Your Own Answer*_____

_____

Q44

What is the test used to detect the presence of antibodies directed against red blood cell antigens?

*Your Own Answer*_____

_____

Q45

Who is the migratory thrombophlebitis associated with malignancy named after?

*Your Own Answer*_____

_____

Correct Answers

A43

Lung carcinoma has increased in death rate in both males and females, probably due to the increased incidence of cigarette smoking.

A44

The Coombs' test is used to look for the presence of antibodies directed against red blood cell antigens.

A45

Migratory thrombophlebitis associated with malignancy is named after Trousseau, who originally diagnosed the condition in himself.

Questions

Q46

What is the most important anatomical component of the blood-air barrier?

*Your Own Answer*_____

Q47

A pH of a solution is 6. What is the concentration of hydroxide ions in the solution?

*Your Own Answer*_____

Q48

Young children should not receive tetracycline therapy because of what side effect?

*Your Own Answer*_____

Correct Answers

A46

The tight junctions between alveolar capillary endothelial cells are the barrier's most important component, because they restrict the movement of macromolecules into the bloodstream from the alveolar wall.

A47

pH + pOH = 14, where pOH = $^-$log(hydroxide ion concentration). In this case, pOH = 14–6 = 8, and so the hydroxide ion concentration is 10^{-8}.

A48

Tetracycline is contraindicated in young children because it can stain their teeth and interfere with tooth development.

Questions

Q49

Mucoid medial degeneration is often seen in patients with which genetic disease?

*Your Own Answer*_____

Q50

A 78-year-old male who resides in a nursing home presents with symptoms of watery diarrhea, dehydration, and malaise. There are no fecal leukocytes or fever. What infectious agent is most likely responsible for this presentation?

*Your Own Answer*_____

Q51

The posterior vaginal fornix lies just anterior to which structure, which can thus be drained of blood or pus using culdocentesis?

*Your Own Answer*_____

Correct Answers

A49

Marfan's syndrome is caused by a defective fibrillin gene, resulting in defects in connective tissue throughout the body. Patients often have mucoid medial degeneration ("cystic medial necrosis"). Mucoid medial degeneration can also be associated with aging and hypertension, as well as arterial aneurysm formation and aortic dissection.

A50

Yersinia enterocolitica would cause crampy abdominal pain, fever, and fecal leukocytes. It causes an invasive, exudative bacterial diarrhea. Enterotoxigenic *E. coli* secretes an exotoxin that induces secretory diarrhea by disrupting intestinal absorption. Clinically, patients present with watery diarrhea, but no fever or abdominal pain.

A51

The posterior vaginal fornix lies just anterior to the rectouterine pouch of Douglas.

Questions

Q52

The Fenton Reaction generates free radicals via what mechanism?

*Your Own Answer*_____

Q53

What is associated with *erythema ab igne?*

*Your Own Answer*_____

Q54

Occlusion of what artery would lead to ischemia in the sino-atrial node in the heart?

*Your Own Answer*_____

Correct Answers

A52

The Fenton Reaction generates the free hydroxyl radical from hydrogen peroxide and transitional metals such as Fe or Cu as described by the following chemical reaction: $Fe^2 + H_2O_2 \longrightarrow Fe^3 + OH^- + OH$.

A53

Erythema ab igne presents with reticulated erythema or reticulated hypopigmented pattern. Usually it happens after prolonged exposure to moderate heat by heating pads or heating blankets.

A54

The SA nodal artery is a terminal branch of the anterior right atrial artery.

Questions

Q55

What class of organism is responsible for creeping eruption?

*Your Own Answer*_____

Q56

Why is atropine useful in treating organophosphate overdoses?

*Your Own Answer*_____

Q57

What organism(s) are associated with botryomycosis?

*Your Own Answer*_____

Correct Answers

A55

The creeping eruption, which is also known as larvae migrans, is caused by larvae of different nematodes. If it is found in the viscera, it is called viscera larvae migrans, and if it is found in the skin, it is called cutaneous larvae migrans. Larvae migrans may be associated with increased eosinophil count.

A56

Organophosphate compounds are inhibitors of anticholinesterase, an enzyme that hydrolyzes acetylcholine. Thus, with an overdose of organophosphate compounds, the transmitter accumulates. Atropine blocks the action of acetylcholine because it competes reversibly with acetylcholine at the muscarinic receptor.

A57

Botryomycosis presents with different areas of ulcerations and sinus tracts with purulent discharge. The discharge is usually yellowish and examination of this discharge will reveal *Staphylococcus aureus* and sometimes *Pseudomonas aeruginosa*. This is really not a fungal infection, but a bacterial infection.

Questions

In the thymus, what causes the formation of Hassal's (thymic) corpuscles?

*Your Own Answer*_____

Q59

What group of bacteria are obligate aerobes, acid-fast, do not stain well by Gram stain, have a relatively slow doubling time, and can cause tuberculosis, leprosy, and swimming pool granulomas?

*Your Own Answer*_____

Q60

What are four important chemotactic factors?

*Your Own Answer*_____

Correct Answers

A58

Degenerating epithelial reticular cells form the Hassal's corpuscles.

A59

Mycobacteria are obligate aerobes. They are acid-fast and stain poorly under Gram stain. Doubling times can be on the order of 20 hours, compared to most bacteria which can double in less than an hour. *M tuberculosis* cause tuberculosis, *M leprae* causes leprosy, and *M marinum* can cause swimming pool granulomas.

A60

Kallikrein, LTB4, C5a, and soluble bacterial products, as well as lymphokines and prostaglandins, are all important chemotactic factors.

Questions

Q61

The right lymphatic duct typically empties into what structure?

*Your Own Answer*_____

Q62

As a result of an automobile accident, a patient has sustained a fracture to the maxilla, just below the orbit. One week later, the patient complains of numbness and tingling sensations in the lower eyelid, lateral side of the nose, upper lip, and skin in the zygomatic region. What structure was probably damaged in the accident?

*Your Own Answer*_____

Q63

What are four drugs used to treat enterobiasis?

*Your Own Answer*_____

Correct Answers

A61

The right lymphatic duct commonly joins the venous system at the junction of the right internal jugular and subclavian vein.

A62

Damage to the infraorbital nerve, located in the maxillary bone, just inferior to the orbital rim, would cause the listed symptoms.

A63

Piperazine, pyrantel pamoate, thiabendazole, and mebendazole are used to treat enterobiasis.

Questions

Q64

Kaposi's sarcoma is a neoplasm most often associated with what disease?

*Your Own Answer*_____

Q65

Gianotti-Crosti syndrome is most commonly assocted with what infectious disease?

*Your Own Answer*_____

Q66

What ligament is lax when the knee is extended?

*Your Own Answer*_____

Correct Answers

A64

Kaposi's sarcoma is associated with HIV infection.

A65

Gianotti-Crosti syndrome is most commonly associated with hepatitis B. It presents with erythematous papules, pruritic erythematous papules, and pustules on the distal extremities and faces of children. It usually lasts about two months.

A66

The posterior cruciate ligament is lax when the knee is extended.

Questions

Q67

What is the Hayflick limit?

*Your Own Answer*_____

Q68

To anesthetize the perineum prior to suturing a laceration, which nerve would be blocked with a local anesthetic?

*Your Own Answer*_____

Q69

What causes oral hairy leukoplakia?

*Your Own Answer*_____

Correct Answers

A67

The Hayflick limit is the limit of time that cells in a culture will live. It was studied and reported by US microbiologist Leonard Hayflick.

A68

The pudendal nerve is the chief sensory nerve of the perineum and thus would be anesthetized in this case.

A69

Oral hairy leukoplakia is a condition that is usually seen on the tongue of HIV-positive patients and is thought to be caused by the Epstein-Barr virus.

Questions

What organism causes Chagas' disease?

*Your Own Answer*_____

A common abnormality of the gastrointestinal tract is the persistence of the remnant of the embryonic yolk stalk, whereby a blind, finger-like pouch projects from the antimesenteric border of the ileum. Since this structure often contains patches of gastric acid-secreting epithelium, the structure may ulcerate and cause intraabdominal bleeding. What is the structural abnormality described above?

*Your Own Answer*_____

A 25-year-old intravenous drug abuser presents with fever, chills, weakness, weight loss, and diaphoresis. On examination, splinter hemorrhages and petechiae are seen. A cardiac murmur is audible on auscultation of the heart. Blood cultures are positive for *Staphylococcus aureus*. For what procedures are antibiotic prophylaxis recommended to prevent infective endocarditis?

*Your Own Answer*_____

Correct Answers

A70

Tyrpansoma cruzi is the causative organism of Chagas' disease. The disease is often seen in South America and acutely causes fever and adenopathy. It also has long-term complications.

A71

Meckel's diverticulum is the structural abnormality described.

A72

Prophylaxis is recommended for esophageal dilation, cystoscopy, bronchoscopy, vaginal hysterectomy, tonsillectomy, prostatic surgery, urethral catheterization, and gallbladder surgery.

Questions

Q73

Cryptococcosis neoformans is typically seen in immunocompromised patients and persons that have heavy exposure to what animal?

*Your Own Answer*_____

Q74

What neoplasm is associated with Peutz-Jeghers syndrome?

*Your Own Answer*_____

Q75

Arteritis, polyarthritis, dermatitis, glomerulone-phritis, retinopathy, and calcinosis in a child is consistent with what diagnosis?

*Your Own Answer*_____

Correct Answers

A73

Heavy exposure to pigeons may lead to cryptococcosis. Cryptococcosis is another deep fungus that has become important in HIV-positive patients. The fungus is found in pigeon excreta and in the soil. It is a small spore.

A74

Peutz-Jeghers syndrome is associated with hyperpigmentation of the skin and mucous membrane, especially the lips. It is also associated with duodenal carcinoma as well as hamartomatous polyps of the intestines. It is inherited as an autosomal dominant disease.

A75

Juvenile dermatomyositis is reported in children and infants. The most important feature is arteritis. However, polyarthritis and dysphagia may be seen. Glomerulonephritis, retinopathy, and calcinosis cutis are also observed.

Questions

Q76

Acute MI is most frequently associated with what type of shock?

*Your Own Answer*_____

_____

Q77

A 92-year-old nursing home resident complained of abdominal pain and vomiting after eating, and a poor appetite. To make the diagnosis of gastroparesis, what test should be performed?

*Your Own Answer*_____

_____

Q78

What type of necrosis is associated with immune-mediated vascular damage?

*Your Own Answer*_____

_____

Correct Answers

A76

Cardiogenic shock often results in acute myocardial infarction.

A77

Scintigraphy with radioisotopic labeled liquid or solid food can demonstrate delayed gastric emptying. If scintigraphy is not available, barium swallow or upper endoscopy can be used to exclude gastric outlet obstruction as the cause for delayed emptying.

A78

Fibrinoid necrosis, characterized by deposition of fibrin-like material in the walls of arteries, is the type of necrosis seen with immune-mediated vascular damage.

Questions

Q79

In general, what is produced by basal ganglia lesions?

*Your Own Answer*_____

Q80

What are three conditions that predispose an individual to gout?

*Your Own Answer*_____

Q81

An extensive infection in the nasal mucosa has resulted in dysfunction of the Bowman's glands in the olfactory area. This would result in a decrease in which type of secretion?

*Your Own Answer*_____

Correct Answers

A79

Lesions will produce hyperkinesia (i.e., tremors, jerky, purposeless involuntary movements, etc.), because projections from the basal ganglia are inhibitory to motor centers of the cortex.

A80

Obesity, diabetes mellitus, hypertension, hyperlipidemia, and arteriosclerosis are all associated with gout.

A81

A dysfunction of the Bowman's glands would result in a decrease in its production of a serous, watery secretion, a medium for solubilizing inhaled odorants.

Questions

Q82

Down's syndrome is associated with a low level of which protein in the maternal amniotic fluid?

*Your Own Answer*_____

_____

Q83

What is the chromosomal abnormality in Klinefelter's syndrome?

*Your Own Answer*_____

_____

Q84

What is the dividing line used in the classification of hemorrhoids as internal or external?

*Your Own Answer*_____

_____

Correct Answers

A82

Down's syndrome (Trisomy 21) is associated with low levels of alpha fetoprotein in maternal amniotic fluid. High levels of alpha fetoprotein are associated with neural tube defects such as spina bifida and anencephaly.

A83

Klinefelter's syndrome, characterized by abnormal sexual development and cognitive defects, is karyotype 47, XXY.

A84

The dentate line is used as the anatomic dividing line for hemorrhoid classification.

Questions

Q85

Thrombosis of the uterine artery, in addition to causing ischemia of the uterus, would also compromise blood flow to which three structures?

*Your Own Answer*_____

Q86

The most common form of leukemia in children originates in which cell type?

*Your Own Answer*_____

Q87

Pancreatic tissue that is found in the small intestine is an example of what?

*Your Own Answer*_____

Correct Answers

A85

The uterine tube, vagina, and cervix would potentially become ischemic following occlusion of the uterine artery.

A86

The most common pediatric malignancy is acute lymphocytic leukemia. Patients usually present with lethargy and fatigue.

A87

Choristoma is normal tissue in the wrong location. This is in contrast to a hamartoma, which is a developmental abnormality composed of disorganized cells or tissue native to that site.

Questions

Q88

The hypophyseal arteries, supplying the pituitary gland, are direct branches of which structure?

*Your Own Answer*_____

Q89

When performing a biopsy of a suspected melanoma on the skin of the upper lip, the incision should be made in which direction in relation to the underlying orbicularis oris muscle?

*Your Own Answer*_____

Q90

What will be the end result of sweat duct obstruction within the stratum corneum?

*Your Own Answer*_____

Correct Answers

A88

The internal carotid artery supplies direct branches to the pituitary gland.

A89

In the face, the wrinkles in the skin run perpendicular to the direction of the fibers of the muscles of facial expression. Thus, the incision should be made within or parallel to the wrinkles (i.e., perpendicular to the muscle fibers).

A90

If the sweat duct obstruction is within the stratum corneum, then it is called miliaria crystallina. If the sweat duct obstruction is further down the epidermis, then it is called miliaria ruba.

Questions

Q91

What is the most common cause of infectious neonatal conjunctivitis?

*Your Own Answer*_____

Q92

Leser-Trélat sign indicates possible malignancy with the sudden appearance of what condition?

*Your Own Answer*_____

Q93

Cinchonism is associated with which drug?

*Your Own Answer*_____

Correct Answers

A91

Chlamydia trachomatis causes an inclusion conjunctivitis in the neonate, which can range from mild to severe.

A92

Multiple seborrheic keratosis

A93

Quinidine, an antiarrhythmic, is the drug associated with cinchonism: Symptoms of cinchonism include ringing in the ears, loss of hearing, and dizziness.

Questions

Q94

A 27-year-old female presents with sudden onset of left-sided hemiparesis. CT scan of the head showed an acute right-sided cerebral infarction. The physician decides to rule out valvular heart disease, which can cause strokes in young adults. What is the most likely valvular cause of embolic stroke in this age group?

*Your Own Answer*_____

Q95

Mutations in DCC, p53, K-ras, and APC occur in what disease of the colon?

*Your Own Answer*_____

Q96

Down's syndrome is associated with an increased risk of developing which type of disease?

*Your Own Answer*_____

Correct Answers

A94

Of the 500,000 new strokes that occur in the U.S., about 5% are in adults below the age of 45. Mitral valve prolapse is a common source of emboli responsible for cerebral strokes in this age group. The best method of detection is a transesophageal echocardiogram. The source of the embolism is fibrin platelet embolization.

A95

In familial adenomatous polyposis of the colon, the adenomatous polyposis coli (APC) gene is mutated, and its loss results in the formation of multiple colonic polyps, which have the potential to become malignant. APC is a tumor suppressor gene along with DCC and p53, which are also inactivated. K-ras, a proto-oncogene, is activated.

A96

Down's syndrome is associated with an increased risk of developing acute leukemias.

Questions

Q97

Rejection of transplanted organs is due primarily to the activity of graft-rejection cells. From what are graft-rejection cells derived?

*Your Own Answer*_____

Q98

What is the source of vaginal lubrication during sexual arousal?

*Your Own Answer*_____

Q99

What is the most common liposarcoma?

*Your Own Answer*_____

Correct Answers

A97

T-lymphocytes give rise to graft-rejection cells.

A98

Lubrication results from diffusion of fluids from venules in the lamina propria.

A99

Myxoid liposarcoma accounts for 45-55% of all liposarcomas. It is characterized by loosely arranged tumor cells with amorphous background material with vacuolated cytoplasm.

Questions

Q100

What are the subcutaneous manifestations of rheumatoid arthritis?

*Your Own Answer*_____

Q101

In contrast to systemic lupus erythematosus, which affects multiple organ systems, discoid lupus affects primarily which organ system?

*Your Own Answer*_____

Q102

An otherwise healthy 29-year-old female presents with painful intercourse which seems to worsen and abate in time with her menses. Pelvic exam demonstrates a fixed and retroverted uterus. What is the most likely diagnosis?

*Your Own Answer*_____

Correct Answers

A100

The subcutaneous manifestations of rheumatoid arthritis include skin atrophy, usually due to steroids; liver palms or Dawson's palms, which are erythema on the palms; yellow coloration of the skin; subcutaneous nodules; episcleritis; lung lesions; and nail ridging.

A101

The effects of discoid lupus are restricted primarily to the skin. Patients present with recurring macular and papular skin lesions. Discoid lupus is differentiated from systemic lupus by the lack of systemic involvement.

A102

Endometriosis is caused by ectopic endometrial tissue outside the uterus. Symptoms include painful intercourse and can often wax and wane with menses.

Questions

Q103

In albinos, what contributes to a lack of skin pigmentation?

*Your Own Answer*_____

Q104

A translocation between chromosomes 9 and 22 is most characteristic of which type of cancer?

*Your Own Answer*_____

Q105

c-sis is an example of what type of factor?

*Your Own Answer*_____

Correct Answers

A103

In tyrosinase (+) albinism, there is normal tyrosinase but a defect in the transport (uptake) of tyrosine into melanocytes. In tyrosinase (-) albinism, the uptake of tyrosine is normal, but a lack of tyrosinase in melanocytes blocks the conversion of tyrosine into melanin pigment.

A104

85% of patients with chronic myelogenous leukemia have a translocation of chromosomes 9 and 22 in which the c-abl proto-oncogene is fused to the bcr gene on 22 and a new 210 kD protein called the Philadelphia chromosome, is formed.

A105

c-sis is a growth factor, which is derived from the PDGF-beta subunit.

Questions

Q106

During allergic reactions and parasitic infections what increases significantly in the affected tissues?

*Your Own Answer*_____

Q107

What drug would be expected to cause gingival hyperplasia (hyperplasia of the gums)?

*Your Own Answer*_____

Q108

What is the name of the triad associated with endothelial injury or damage, hypercoagulability of blood, imbalance of prothrombotic and antithrombotic factors, and stasis?

*Your Own Answer*_____

Correct Answers

A106

Allergic reactions and parasitic infections characteristically are associated with an increase in the numbers of eosinophils.

A107

Phenytoin is an anticonvulsant, which causes gingival hyperplasia as a side effect. Other side effects of this agent include bone loss and hirsutism.

A108

Virchow's triad is used to describe the conditions that promote the formation of thrombi. They include stasis, endothelial damage or injury, hypercoagulability of blood, and imbalance of factors that are prothrombotic and antithrombotic (which may promote the hypercoagulability of blood).

Questions

Q109

What anaerobic organism might be commonly found in an intraabdominal abscess?

*Your Own Answer*_____

Q110

A 58-year-old man came in to the physician's office for a routine physical exam. His history and exam was unremarkable except for an unusual bluish-black pigmentation over his face and fingers. Adding sodium hydroxide to his urine sample turned the specimen black. Spinal films revealed intervertebral disk spaces showing greater radiodensity than the adjacent vertebrae. What is the diagnosis?

*Your Own Answer*_____

Q111

The cells of the theca interna secrete what substance, which is then converted to estradiol by the granulosa cells of an ovarian follicle?

*Your Own Answer*_____

Correct Answers

A109

Bacteroides fragilis is a common anaerobic pathogen in intraabdominal abscess.

A110

Ochronosis (also known as alkaptonuria) is an autosomal recessive trait characterized by deficiency in homogentisic acid oxidase, an enzyme that is necessary for the metabolism of phenylalanine and tyrosine. Ochronosis can produce ankylosis of joints and other cartilaginous structures. Darkening of the skin is present, which represents deposits of homogentisic acid in cartilage and the dermis. Porphyria cutanea tarda also causes skin discoloration.

A111

Androstenedione, an androgen, is initially synthesized by the theca interna, but it diffuses into the follicle to be converted to estradiol (estrogen) by the granulosa cells.

Questions

Q112

Clostridium difficile entercolitis is most commonly associated with the use of what class of drugs?

*Your Own Answer*_____

_____

Q113

What is a treatment for psoriasis?

*Your Own Answer*_____

_____

Q114

A 28-year-old woman had a dry cough that had been worsening for five months. She went to the hospital because of an acute bout of coughing associated with hemoptysis. A chest X ray and follow-up CT scan of the lungs revealed a large anterior mediastinum mass. What types of neoplasms may present with an anterior mediastinum mass?

*Your Own Answer*_____

_____

Correct Answers

A112

Broad-spectrum antibiotics eliminate normal bowel flora, allowing overgrowth of other organisms including *Clostridium difficile*. *C. difficile* produces a toxin causing enterocolitis.

A113

Psoriasis has different treatments depending on its severity. Topical steroids are well known for treatment of psoriasis. Cyclosporine and methotrexate are also used as immune modulators for treatment of psoriasis. Recently, topical vitamin D derivative (Dovonex) has been approved by the FDA for psoriasis treatment.

A114

10% of primary mediastinal neoplasms are thymomas. They usually present anteriorly, and 25% are found to be malignant. Retrosternal thyroid tumors can present as an anterior, superior, and middle mediastinal mass. Germ cell tumors, bronchogenic cysts, aortic aneurysms, and pericardial cysts can all present as anterior mediastinal masses.

Questions

Q115

Regarding the base content of DNA, what does A equal?

*Your Own Answer*_____

Q116

What are the risk factors for breast cancer?

*Your Own Answer*_____

Q117

What is the inheritance of lipoid proteinosis?

*Your Own Answer*_____

Correct Answers

A115

In DNA, the pyrimidine content must equal the purine content. This is because a purine base (adenine (A), guanine (G)) is always paired with a pyrimidine base (cytosine (C), thymine (T)). Furthermore, A pairs with T and G pairs with C. Thus A = T.

A116

Late age at first full-term pregnancy is a risk factor of breast cancer, as well as early menarche and nulliparity. Long duration of oral contraceptive use also contributes to an increase risk of developing breast cancer. The risk is greater in women with histological evidence of ductal hyperplasia. History of breast cancer in a first-degree relative increases a woman's risk for breast cancer 1.5-3.0 fold.

A117

It is autosomal recessive. Lipoid proteinosis, or Urbach-Weithe disease, presents with hyaline deposits under the skin and the mucosa. It can affect the buccal mucosa, as well as the throat and vocal cords.

Questions

Q118

A 50-year-old male has a chronic, recurrent disorder. He presents with a well-marginated, erythematous plaque with silvery-white surface scales on his elbow. He also has arthritis and onycholysis with pitting of the nail plate. What is the most likely diagnosis?

*Your Own Answer*_____

Q119

Organophosphate poisoning inhibits which enzyme?

*Your Own Answer*_____

Q120

What is the name of the classification system for cardiac antiarrhythmic drugs?

*Your Own Answer*_____

Correct Answers

A118

Psoriasis is a chronic nonpruritic skin disorder associated with arthritis, pitting of the nails, and thickening of the nail plate with accumulation of subungual debris. Its distribution includes extensor surfaces such as knees, elbows, and buttocks.

A119

Aceytlcholinesterase is inhibited in organophosphate poisoning, leading to increased levels of acetylcholine. Symptoms of this poisoning include nausea, vomiting, and confusion.

A120

There are four Vaughn Williams classes, based on mechanism of action.

Questions

Q121

A 24-year-old male with a history of intravenous drug abuse and unprotected sex presents with weight loss, fever, and lymphadenopathy. His physician suspects AIDS. If she is correct, which infection is she most likely to find in her patient?

*Your Own Answer*_____

Q122

What animal is associated with echinococcosis?

*Your Own Answer*_____

Q123

Deficiency of vitamin A would be associated with what common symptom?

*Your Own Answer*_____

Correct Answers

A121

Pneumocystis carinii pneumonia is an opportunistic infection in immunocompromised individuals. It is the most common infection in patients with AIDS. Individuals usually present with shortness of breath and hypoxemia.

A122

Echinococcosis is caused by tapeworms of dogs. The skin findings are usually urticaria. They also cause hydatid cyst of the liver.

A123

Deficiency of vitamin A might lead to night blindness. Vitamin A is involved in synthesis of rhodopsin.

Questions

Q124

Which fungus most commonly causes meningitis in AIDS patients?

*Your Own Answer*_____

Q125

A newborn presents with microcephaly, round facies, and a characteristic cat cry. What is the most likely genetic defect?

*Your Own Answer*_____

Q126

In areas of the brain where there is no blood-brain barrier, what do the capillaries lack?

*Your Own Answer*_____

Correct Answers

A124

Cryptococcal meningitis is often seen in patients with AIDS. Cryptococcus is a fungus that causes opportunistic infection in AIDS patients.

A125

Deletion of the short arm of chromosome 5 (5p-) leads to the Cri du Chat syndrome ("cat cry") because infants up to one year have a characteristic cry like a cat. They also present with microcephaly, round facies, and severe mental retardation.

A126

Areas of the brain with no blood-brain barrier (i.e., area postrema) have capillaries that lack tight junctions between adjacent endothelial cells.

Questions

Q127

A 25-year-old male was brought to the emergency room by paramedics because of smoke inhalation. He is unconscious and his lips and nail beds are cherry-red. His carboxyhemoglobin level is 60%. Later on, lung auscultation revealed ronchi, and this patient was diagnosed with respiratory failure. What would be the most immediate intervention?

*Your Own Answer*_____

Q128

What is the role of T-cell lymphocytes?

*Your Own Answer*_____

Q129

What is the primary source of the lipids in the lymph in the thoracic duct?

*Your Own Answer*_____

Correct Answers

A127

The most immediate concern for patients suffering from smoke inhalation is to overcome loss of ventilation induced by CO, which damages lung tissue. Patients should be given 100% O_2 immediately by a tight-fitting mask or intubation. This patient may also require hyperbaric O_2 therapy, as indicated by a very high carboxyhemoglobin concentration.

A128

T-cell lymphocytes are involved in the cytotoxic response to certain antigens (e.g. poison ivy), producing a hypersensitivity reaction. T-cells are also responsible for graft rejection, because they are able to recognize the class I MHC molecule of allografts.

A129

The lipids are derived from the absorption of triglycerides in the central lacteals of intestinal villi.

Questions

Q130

During thyroidectomy, the inferior thyroid veins are ligated just proximal to where they join which vessels?

*Your Own Answer*_____

Q131

What do steroid-producing cells characteristically contain in their cytoplasm?

*Your Own Answer*_____

Q132

A patient with Crohn's disease forms an abnormal connection between her colon and her vagina due to her disease. How is such a connection best described?

*Your Own Answer*_____

Correct Answers

A130

The inferior thyroid veins, when paired, usually drain into the left and right brachiocephalic veins. When there is only one inferior thyroid vein, most of the time it drains into the left brachiocephalic vein. In either case, the veins would have to be identified and ligated prior to removal of the gland.

A131

Steroid-producing cells contain an abundance of smooth endoplasmic reticulum. They also typically exhibit mitochondria with tubular cristae and lipid droplets in the cytoplasm.

A132

A fistula is an abnormal connection between two organs or structures.

Questions

Q133

Patients with Down's syndrome are especially likely to develop what type of cancer?

*Your Own Answer*_____

_____

Q134

What diseases are associated with pyoderma gangrenosum?

*Your Own Answer*_____

_____

Q135

What is the myeloproliferative disorder characterized by excessive red blood cell production?

*Your Own Answer*_____

_____

Correct Answers

A133

Patients with Down's syndrome, Trisomy 21, have a greater susceptibility to acute leukemia.

A134

Pyoderma gangrenosum is an ulcerating condition of the skin, which is usually associated with inflammatory bowel diseases, such as ulcerative colitis and Crohn's disease, as well as rheumatoid arthritis and leukemia.

A135

Polycythemia vera is the myeloproliferative disorder characterized by excessive red blood cell production. It can be associated with decreased erythropoietin (primary p. vera) or increased erythropoietin (chronic hypoxia, tumors with endocrine activity).

Questions

Q136

A 26-year-old African-American man has a benign skin lesion removed. Six months later, he presents with a large, hypertrophic mass of tissue, which appears to be invading surrounding normal tissue. The biopsy specimen is significant only for scar tissue. What is this lesion referred to as?

*Your Own Answer*_____

Q137

What is directly related to the inferior surface of the prostate gland?

*Your Own Answer*_____

Q138

What organ system is most often affected in sarcoidosis?

*Your Own Answer*_____

Correct Answers

A136

Keloids are exuberant masses of scar tissue most commonly found in African-Americans.

A137

The urogenital diaphragm is anatomically related to the inferior surface of the prostate gland.

A138

The respiratory system is affected in 90% of cases. The typical lesion is a non-caseating granuloma. Any organ system may be affected in sarcoidosis, however.

Questions

Q139

What would be the classification of a vessel that contains an internal elastic membrane, external elastic membrane, and a tunica media with 20 layers of smooth muscle?

*Your Own Answer*_____

Q140

What is the function of satellite cells associated with skeletal muscle fibers?

*Your Own Answer*_____

Q141

When doing a "chest tap," where should the needle be inserted (relative to a rib) to avoid damage to the intercostal nerve and/or artery and gain easy access to the pleural cavity?

*Your Own Answer*_____

Correct Answers

A139

The characteristics listed describe a typical medium (muscular) artery.

A140

When a muscle is injured, satellite cells proliferate and participate in regeneration of skeletal muscle.

A141

Since the intercostal nerve and vessels run just deep to the inferior border of their respective rib, a needle should always be inserted just superior to the superior border of a rib to avoid damage to these structures.

Questions

Q142

What is the infectious agent implicated in the development of Burkitt's lymphoma?

*Your Own Answer*_____

Q143

A 23-year-old asthmatic presents with an exacerbation of his asthma and a low-grade fever. Sputum examination demonstrates eosinophilia and Curschmann's spirals (mucoid casts). Blood examination reveals eosinophilia. What is the most likely cause of this disorder?

*Your Own Answer*_____

Q144

What causes "rose spots"?

*Your Own Answer*_____

Correct Answers

A142

Epstein-Barr virus, in addition to causing infectious mononucleosis, has been implicated in the development of Burkitt's lymphoma.

A143

Aspergillus fumigatus is the most likely cause. This organism causes eosinophilic pneumonia in asthma patients through an allergic reaction to its antigens.

A144

Rose spots are classical as a cutaneous sign for salmonella infection. There are three primary species: *Salmonella typhi, Salmonella choleraesuis,* and *Salmonella enteritides.* Cutaneous eruption starts about seven to ten days after the high fever, with slightly raised erythematous nontender papules.

Questions

Q145

What is the process of inactivation of one X chromosome in female cells to become a Barr body?

*Your Own Answer*_____

Q146

What is the inheritance pattern for incontinenta pigmenti?

*Your Own Answer*_____

Q147

What is a severe form of seborrheic dermatitis seen in infants?

*Your Own Answer*_____

Correct Answers

A145

Lyonization is the inactivation of one X chromosome in each female cell. The resulting inactive chromatin is referred to as a Barr body.

A146

X-linked dominant diseases are very rare. Those are Child's syndrome, focal dermal hepoplasia (Goltz syndrome), and incontinenta pigmenta.

A147

A severe form, occurring in infancy, is known as Loiner's disease.

Questions

Q148

A 32-year-old HIV-positive female presents with low-grade fever, severe perianal pain, and previous history of herpetic vulvovaginal lesions. What are likely causes of anal lesions in AIDS?

*Your Own Answer*_____

Q149

What would a surgical biopsy specimen of the normal appendix display?

*Your Own Answer*_____

Q150

What explains the effects of carbon monoxide poisoning?

*Your Own Answer*_____

Correct Answers

A148

Anal herpetic ulcers affect both women and men and are associated with anal-receptive intercourse. Cytomegalovirus is found in human cervical secretions, semen, saliva, feces, and blood for months after exposure. It can be transmitted sexually; consequently, anal intercourse can result in perirectal CMV lesions.

A149

The appendix typically has an abundance of lymphatic nodules with active germinal centers.

A150

Carbon monoxide demonstrates much higher affinity for hemoglobin than does oxygen. As such, it leads to hypoxic injury.

Questions

Q151

Prior to surgical removal of a uterine tube, its blood supply, derived from which arteries, would be ligated?

*Your Own Answer*_____

Q152

An aneurysm in the posterior wall of the superior mesenteric artery 1 cm from its origin would likely compress which structure?

*Your Own Answer*_____

Q153

Which genetic abnormality is associated with Burkitt's lymphoma?

*Your Own Answer*_____

Correct Answers

A151

The uterine tube is supplied by branches derived from the uterine artery and the ovarian artery.

A152

The superior mesenteric artery crosses directly anterior to the left renal vein, and thus the aneurysm would likely compress this vessel.

A153

Burkitt's lymphoma, in addition to being associated with Epstein-Barr virus infection, has been linked to a translocation between chromosomes 8 and 14.

Questions

Q154

Wernicke-Korsakoff syndrome results from deficiency of which substance?

*Your Own Answer*_____

Q155

What is an example of a protease inhibitor that acts as an anticoagulant?

*Your Own Answer*_____

Q156

Histologically, how would the anterior interventricular coronary artery be classified?

*Your Own Answer*_____

Correct Answers

A154

Vitamin B1 deficiency may cause Wernicke-Korsakoff syndrome, which is characterized by degeneration of the brain stem and other areas and results in confusion and ataxia. Deficiency of this same vitamin causes beriberi.

A155

α2-macroglobulin is a protease inhibitor that acts as an anticoagulant in the coagulation and fibrinolysis cascade.

A156

The anterior interventricular artery is a medium (muscular) artery.

Questions

Q157

What is pathognomonic of lichen planus?

*Your Own Answer*_____

Q158

What is the most common type of embolism?

*Your Own Answer*_____

Q159

Your patient has a stab wound in the left 5th intercostal space, 9 cm from the midline of the sternum. What structure is most likely to be damaged?

*Your Own Answer*_____

Correct Answers

A157

Wickham's striae is a network of white lines on the lichen planus papules. It is thought to be caused by a focal increase in the thickness of the granular layer and of the total epidermis.

A158

Thromboembolism is the most common type of embolism (99%). Thromboembolism may be caused by stasis, endothelial damage or injury, or hypercoagulability of blood that results in a thrombus, which resolves by embolization or breaking loose with subsequent obstruction downstream.

A159

The apex of the heart is most often located at the level of the left 5th intercostal space, about 9 cm from the midline.

Questions

Q160
Your patient is a 12-year-old girl who is exhibiting various male secondary sex characteristics (i.e., facial hair, deep voice, etc.). She may have a tumor of what structure, causing an overproduction of dehydroepiandrosterone?

*Your Own Answer*_____

Q161
What medication is indicated for dermatitis herpetiformis?

*Your Own Answer*_____

Q162
A blood disorder that involves a decrease in the number of circulating platelets would be related to what type of disfunction?

*Your Own Answer*_____

Correct Answers

A160

The zona reticularis of the adrenal cortex secretes androgens, so an increase in its activity
(i.e, a hormone-secreting tumor) would cause an
appearance of male secondary sex characteristics in a female.

A161

Dapsone is the indicated treatment for dermatitis herpetiformis, which is a neutrophilic, sub-
epidermal, blister-forming disease of the skin.

A162

A dysfunction of megakaryocytes, platelets re-
siding in bone marrow, would be related to this
blood disorder.

Questions

Q163

Pathologic examination of bone from a patient with Paget's disease of bone (osteitis deformans) would demonstrate what histologic feature?

*Your Own Answer*_____

Q164

When making a surgical incision in the abdominal wall, what layer of the superficial fascia would be encountered immediately deep to the skin?

*Your Own Answer*_____

Q165

Multiple sclerosis, which involves significant demyelination in the central nervous system, is primarily a disease of which cells?

*Your Own Answer*_____

Correct Answers

A163

Paget's disease of bone is characterized by increased vascular supply and abnormal bone formation. It leads to deformity and fracture. The increased vascular supply can lead to high output heart failure.

A164

The superficial fascia of the anterior abdominal wall is subdivided into a loose, fatty layer known as Camper's fascia, and a deeper membranous layer called Scarpa's fascia. Camper's fascia would be cut first in a surgical incision.

A165

Oligodendrocytes, the myelin-forming cells of the central nervous system, are severely affected in multiple sclerosis.

Questions

Q166

In what vascular disease would immune complexes, antineutrophil autoantibodies, fibrinoid necrosis, and thrombosis be present?

*Your Own Answer*_____

Q167

Which enzyme is responsible for the inactivation of penicillin class antibiotics?

*Your Own Answer*_____

Q168

What antibody class is involved in the secondary response to an antigen?

*Your Own Answer*_____

Correct Answers

A166

Classic polyarteritis nodosa is a vasculitis which affects the small-and medium-sized arteries of the systemic circulation. The acute phase presents with fibrinoid necrosis, immune complexes, antineutrophil autoantibodies (or ANCAs), and thrombosis.

A167

Beta-lactamase is a penicillin-binding protein that hydrolyzes penicillin compounds to inactivate them.

A168

IgG is the main antibody produced in the secondary response to an antigen. It is very important in opsonization (enhancement of phagocytosis) of bacteria.

Questions

Q169

Hyaline sclerosis, microaneurysm formation, fibrinoid necrosis, and intimal thickening are likely to occur in small muscular arteries and arterioles during which disease?

*Your Own Answer*_____

Q170

Which enzyme is utilized by retroviruses for transcribing their RNA to DNA?

*Your Own Answer*_____

Q171

Absorption of radiation of 400 rads is likely to most severely affect which system in the human body?

*Your Own Answer*_____

Correct Answers

A169

Atherosclerosis

A170

Retroviruses are RNA viruses that use reverse transcriptase to make DNA.

A171

The hematopoietic syndrome occurs when 200-600 rads of radiation are absorbed, and is characterized by mild Gl symptoms, which develop into changes in the peripheral blood and atrophy of the lymph nodes, spleen, and bone marrow. The lymphocytes are depressed first, followed by depression of neutrophils, platelets, and red blood cells.

Questions

Q172

A 12-year-old boy is brought to the emergency department at midnight with pain in the periumbilical region. Palpation of the abdomen reveals that the point of maximum tenderness is between the navel and the anterior superior iliac spine in the right lower quadrant. What is the most likely diagnosis?

*Your Own Answer*_____

Q173

When blood levels of luteinizing hormone drop, the granulosa lutein cells exhibit a concomitant drop in what type of production?

*Your Own Answer*_____

Q174

A 64-year-old female complains of substernal chest pain radiating down her left arm. Upon arriving at the emergency room, she was found to have elevated ST-T wave segments in the anteriorlateral leads on the EKG. Her cpk enzymes were elevated, and the physician diagnosed her as having a myocardial infarction. This patient was postmenopausal and a diabetic. She also has chronic hypertension. What treatments are recommended after a heart attack in this patient?

*Your Own Answer*_____

Correct Answers

A172

The signs described are most often associated with acute appendicitis. Since pain fibers from the appendix enter the spinal cord at T10, pain is often initially referred to the periumbilical region. Because of the subsequent local irritation of the parietal peritoneum by the inflamed appendix, the severe pain is then localized to McBurney's point, two-thirds of the way between the umbilicus and anterior superior iliaci spine.

A173

The granulosa lutein cells of the corpus luteum produce progesterone under the influence of luteinizing hormone (LH).

A174

Aspirin is highly recommended for prophylaxis after a stroke or myocardial infarction to reduce the incidence of further thrombosis. Tight control of diabetes mellitus in a patient with coronary artery disease is necessary to prevent further atherosclerosis and recurrent MI. Postmenopausal estrogen has been shown to increase the HDL and, thus, decrease the risk for coronary artery disease.

Questions

Q175

The isthmus of the thyroid gland lies just anterior to which structure?

*Your Own Answer*_____

Q176

A 38-year-old female presents suddenly with left-side hemiparesis. CT scan of the brain reveals right-sided embolic stroke. Her past medical history is significant for a prosthetic mitral valve secondary to rheumatic heart disease. Her physician suspects endocarditis. What organism is probably responsible for endocarditis in this patient?

*Your Own Answer*_____

Q177

Cyclosporine adversely affects the functioning of what organ system?

*Your Own Answer*_____

Correct Answers

A175

A consistent anatomical landmark for the isthmus of the thyroid gland is the level of the 2nd to 4th tracheal rings.

A176

The prevalence of a stroke ranges from 15-20% from prosthetic valve endocarditis and is especially high in patients with *Staphylococcus aureus* endocarditis. *Streptococcus pneumoniae* can cause endocarditis, but staphylococcus is more common. *Streptococcus pneumoniae* is a common cause of community-acquired pneumonia.

A177

Cyclosporine is a new immunosuppressant, which is used in prevention and treatment of transplant rejection and treatment of psoriasis and other skin diseases. The major adverse effect of cyclosporine is renal (kidney) toxicity.

Questions

Q178

A patient has a gunshot wound to the chest. X rays reveal that the bullet is lodged in a structure that lies directly posterior to the hilus (root) of the right lung. What structure is the bullet likely lodged in?

*Your Own Answer*_____

Q179

The cutaneous eruption that disappears by the end of two to three days, clearing from the face, is characteristic of what infection?

*Your Own Answer*_____

Q180

A 42-year-old man presents with weakness, dyspnea on exertion and mid-thoracic back pain. On physical examination, he was found to have vertebral tenderness on palpation and pallor. Laboratory data revealed hypercalcemia, anemia, elevation of the erythrocyte sedimentation rate, and an elevated creatinine level. A bone marrow reveals plasma cells predominantly. His physician suspects multiple myeloma. What tests can be used to aid in the diagnosis?

*Your Own Answer*_____

Correct Answers

A178

The esophagus lies directly posterior to the root of the right lung.

A179

The rubella eruption disappears by the end of two to three days, clearing from the face.

A180

A diagnosis is based on an M spike seen on serum electrophoresis plus any of three additional findings: elevated bone marrow plasma cells, detected by bone marrow biopsy, "pushed out" bone lesions, detected by a skeletal radiographic survey, or Bence-Jones proteinuria.

Questions

An obese 48-year-old female presents with new onset diabetes. Her physician's diagnosis is syndrome X. What symptoms were probably found in this patient?

*Your Own Answer*_____

In the scalp, which tissue layer is the most vascular, and is thus the source of profuse bleeding associated with scalp lacerations?

*Your Own Answer*_____

A five-year-old child whose family lives in a dilapidated house presents with lethargy and cognitive deficits. The mother reports that from time to time the child ingests paint chips. What is the most likely diagnosis?

*Your Own Answer*_____

Correct Answers

A181

Syndrome X represents a cluster of cardiovascular risk factors such as glucose intolerance, hypertension, coronary artery disease, dyslipidemia, and obesity. It is mainly associated with insulin resistance.

A182

The dense connective tissue layer is the most vascular in the scalp. The vessels themselves are tightly bound to collagen fibers in the surrounding tissue, which prevents collapse and retraction of vessels following a laceration, resulting in extensive bleeding.

A183

This child's history and symptoms are typical of lead poisoning.

Questions

Q184

What is the most common immunologic abnormality in ataxia-telangiectasia?

*Your Own Answer*_____

Q185

Multiple myeloma tumors arise from what immune cell?

*Your Own Answer*_____

Q186

Where does erythema nodosum usually manifest symptoms?

*Your Own Answer*_____

Correct Answers

A184

Ataxia-telangiectasia is an autosomal recessive disease. In addition to ataxia and telangiectasia patients also have recurrent sinus and pulmonary infections. They have increased alpha fetoprotein and IgA deficiency. They also present scleroderma-like skin findings as well as atopica dermatitis, café au lait macules, and cutaneous malignancies.

A185

Multiple myelomas arise from plasma cells that are antibody-producing, activated B cells. Multiple myelomas produce Bence-Jones proteins (free immunoglobulin light chains) and cause osteolytic lesions.

A186

Erythema nodosum is tender erythematous nodules, usually on the lower legs of young women. It has multiple causes, such as sarcoidosis, pregnancy, oral contraceptives, strep throat among others.

Questions

Q187

A patient is diagnosed as having an aneurysm of the middle cerebral artery. The aneurysm resulted from a defect in which structure?

*Your Own Answer*_____

Q188

What test is necessary before Pimozide treatment?

*Your Own Answer*_____

Q189

What is the primary event that occurs in the vessel leading to atherosclerosis?

*Your Own Answer*_____

Correct Answers

A187

Aneurysms result from weakening in the tunica media of arteries, often where atherosclerotic lesions destroy the smooth muscle and elastic connective tissue in the tunica media.

A188

Pimozide may cause some EKG changes, such as prolonged QT-intervals. This is why a baseline EKG is necessary to monitor the patient. Pimozide is an anti-psychotic drug, which blocks the dopaminergic receptors in the central nervous system. It is used in Tourette's disorder as well as in delusions of parasitosis.

A189

The primary event in atherosclerosis is endothelial injury, which leads to the attraction of monocytes and platelets. Platelets aggregate, thrombosis occurs, and then monocytes and platelets release factors that initiate smooth muscle migration and proliferation, as well as extracellular matrix synthesis.

Questions

Q190

In humans, during the normal resting state, most of the blood glucose is consumed by which organ?

*Your Own Answer*_____

Q191

What disease is associated with Argyll-Robertson pupil?

*Your Own Answer*_____

Q192

What organism is evident under Woods lamp?

*Your Own Answer*_____

Correct Answers

A190

The brain consumes an average of 120 g of glucose per day, which is about 60% of the glucose utilization of the body. Other tissues rely more heavily on other energy substrates (e.g., fatty acids).

A191

Syphilis causes Argyle-Robertson pupil, which is when the pupil accommodates, but does not react.

A192

Corynebacteria is the pathogenic agent in erythrasma, which reveals violaceous erythema under the Woods lamp.

Questions

Q193

Which organism is usually associated with the toxin that can lead to the development of toxic shock syndrome?

*Your Own Answer*_____

Q194

Where are aged and damaged red blood cells destroyed primarily by macrophages?

*Your Own Answer*_____

Q195

During thyroidectomy, the superior thyroid artery is ligated. Care must be taken not to include the nearby external laryngeal nerve in the ligature, otherwise, which muscle will be paralyzed?

*Your Own Answer*_____

Correct Answers

A193

S*taphylococcus aureus* is a Gram-positive organism that produces the exotoxin, which leads to toxic shock syndrome. Tampon use has been identified as a risk factor for development of the syndrome.

A194

The spleen is a primary site of destruction of red blood cells.

A195

The cricothyroid muscle is innervated by the superior laryngeal branch of the vagus nerve.

Questions

Q196

Deficiency of what vitamin is most likely to produce a bleeding disorder?

*Your Own Answer*_____

Q197

Which structure transports oxygen-rich blood toward the fetal heart?

*Your Own Answer*_____

Q198

A three-year-old child develops enteritis. Shortly after, the child develops hemolytic-uremic syndrome (thrombocytopenia, hemolysis, and acute renal failure). What is the most likely causative organism of the enteritis?

*Your Own Answer*_____

Correct Answers

A196

Vitamin K is involved in synthesis of clotting factors. Deficiency leads to bleeding disorders.

A197

The ductus venosus, a continuation of the left umbilical vein through the fetal liver, carries oxygenated maternal blood (plus venous blood from the fetal portal vein) toward the fetal heart.

A198

Escherichia coli causes enteritis and has also been linked to the development of hemolytic-uremic syndrome. Reaction to toxin may trigger disseminated intravascular coagulation, leading to renal failure.

Questions

Q199

What would be the result of a lesion that destroys both inferior colliculi?

*Your Own Answer*_____

Q200

What necrosis type would be expected in a lesion caused by tuberculosis?

*Your Own Answer*_____

Q201

Pleural and peritoneal mesotheliomas are related to exposure to what substance?

*Your Own Answer*_____

Correct Answers

A199

Deafness would result from the destruction of the inferior colliculi, because they would be unable to relay auditory signals to higher levels of the auditory system (e.g., medial geniculate, auditory cortex).

A200

Caseous necrosis is the type of necrosis seen in granulomatous diseases such as tuberculosis.

A201

Asbestos has been linked to the development of pleural and peritoneal mesotheliomas, as well as to lung cancer.

Questions

Q202

Under what conditions is coagulative necrosis found?

*Your Own Answer*_____

_____

Q203

What tests should be regularly checked during Accutane treatment?

*Your Own Answer*_____

_____

Q204

A patient presents with weakness and loss of fine, skilled movements of the extremities on one side of the body. Where is the damage?

*Your Own Answer*_____

_____

Correct Answers

A202

Coagulative necrosis is a type of cell death, which is characterized by the maintenance of cell outlines with the denaturation of proteins. It occurs due to ischemia, infarction, hypoxia, and toxic injury.

A203

Accutane is used for cystic acne. Accutane has side effects on the liver (liver function tests) and it may increase triglycerides and cholesterol. Also, because of the teratogenic effect, a pregnancy test is strongly recommended.

A204

Damage would be in the lateral corticospinal tract in the cervical cord, the chief descending motor pathway that controls skilled voluntary movements of the extremities.

Questions

Q205

The pain from myocardial ischemia reaches the spinal cord via which structure?

*Your Own Answer*_____

Q206

A defect leading to decreased epithelial chloride transport is characteristic of which disease?

*Your Own Answer*_____

Q207

What gland type is associated with Fox-Fordyce disease?

*Your Own Answer*_____

Correct Answers

A205

The cardiac branches of the sympathetic trunk, in addition to supplying sympathetic motor innervation to the heart, also carry the sensory fibers mediating pain from the myocardium.

A206

Cystic fibrosis, the most common autosomal recessive disease in Caucasian children, is caused by a defect in epithelial chloride transport in exocrine glands. The affected children present with recurrent pulmonary infections and pancreatic insufficiency.

A207

Fox-Fordyce disease presents with small discrete papules, usually on the axilla, and is commonly seen in women. It is related to the apocrine glands.

Questions

Q208

CREST syndrome includes what five features?

*Your Own Answer*_____

Q209

What is the most common soft tissue tumor?

*Your Own Answer*_____

Q210

A patient with osteitis fibrosa cystica exhibits fibrous degeneration of bone with removal of bone matrix. This would relate to what type of increased activity?

*Your Own Answer*_____

Correct Answers

A208

CREST syndrome includes calcinosis cutis, Raynaud's phenomenon, esophageal dysfunction, sclerodactyly, and telangiectasia. It is a variant of scleroderma.

A209

Lipoma usually becomes apparent between 40 and 60 years of age and is the most common soft tissue tumor.

A210

Osteitis fibrosa cystica, usually resulting from hyperparathyroidism, involves increased activity of osteoclasts, and thus bone resorption and increased blood calcium levels.

Questions

What anti-malarial drug should not be given with gold?

*Your Own Answer*_____

Q212

The median umbilical ligament extends from the apex of the bladder to the umbilicus. Which structure is contained in this ligament?

*Your Own Answer*_____

Q213

A patient with a tumor in the root of the neck develops difficulty in breathing. Examination shows that the trachea is patent. What is another possible cause of this problem?

*Your Own Answer*_____

Correct Answers

A211

Chloroquine

A212

The urachus, a remnant of the embryonic allantois, lies in the median umbilical ligament.

A213

Damage to the phrenic nerve would paralyze the ipsilateral hemidiaphragm, resulting in respiratory distress.

Questions

Q214

DNA synthesis occurs in which cell cycle phase?

*Your Own Answer*_____

Q215

A 19-year-old woman presented with a painful, diffuse erythematous rash. A low-grade fever and sore throat had been present for several days. Two weeks earlier, the patient had been given trimethoprim-sulfamethoxazole for an upper respiratory tract infection. On exam, there was blotchy erythema on the patient's trunk and proximal extremities as well as crusting of the lips. What is the most likely diagnosis?

*Your Own Answer*_____

Q216

A 26-year-old female presents with new-onset seizures. Arteriography shows a localized lesion with dilated vascular structures but no tumor. Which histologic feature would you expect to be missing in this lesion?

*Your Own Answer*_____

Correct Answers

A214

DNA synthesis occurs in cell cycle phase S. The G_0 (Gap 0) is a resting phase where the cell cycle is stopped. G_1 (Gap 1) phase is also a resting phase, but it is actively part of the cell division cycle. After G_1, DNA replication occurs in the S phase followed by the G_2 phase, in which proteins and RNA are produced. Finally, cell division or mitosis occurs in the M phase.

A215

Toxic epidermal necrolysis is a life-threatening idiosyncratic, exfoliative disease of the skin and mucous membranes that presents with epidermal detachment from the dermis. The agents most commonly associated with toxic epidermal necrolysis are sulfonamides, anticonvulsants, and nonsteroidal anti-inflammatory agents.

A216

This patient has an arteriovenous malformation. In this structure, arterial and venous structures connect directly without capillaries. One would expect to find both arterioles and venules.

Questions

Q217

In humans, what is a precursor of bile salts, steroids hormones, and vitamin D?

Your Own Answer_____

Q218

A 54-year-old male recovering alcoholic who is also being treated with Coumadin for deep-vein thrombosis develops an elevated prothrombin time after being prescribed a new medication as part of his rehabilitation. What is most likely to be the new drug?

Your Own Answer_____

Q219

What antibody class is the main antibody in secretions (e.g., saliva)?

Your Own Answer_____

Correct Answers

A217

Cholesterol is a precursor of bile salts, steroids hormones, and vitamin D. Cholesterol can become cholecalciferol (vitamin D_3) in the presence of sunlight.

A218

Disulfiram is a drug used in alcohol rehabilitation, which causes acute illness on ingestion of alcohol. It is metabolized by the hepatic cytochrome P450 system and so can interact with warfarin, which is metabolized by the same system.

A219

IgA is the main immunoglobulin in secretions like saliva, tears, and gastrointestinal secretions. IgA can exist in a monomeric or dimeric form.

Questions

Q220

A bullet has grazed the posterior surface of the heart, and venous blood is slowly accumulating in the pericardial sac. The bullet grazed the heart at the level of the atrioventricular groove. What structure was probably nicked by the bullet?

*Your Own Answer*_____

Q221

What cancer "never" metastasizes?

*Your Own Answer*_____

Q222

When repairing an indirect inguinal hernia, what nerve is vulnerable to damage because of its relationship to the inguinal canal?

*Your Own Answer*_____

Correct Answers

A220

The coronary sinus, carrying most of the venous blood of the myocardium, runs in the atrioventricular groove on the posterior side of the heart, and thus, may have been nicked.

A221

Basal cell carcinoma does not metastasize. It is locally destructive.

A222

The ilioinguinal nerve, supplying cutaneous innervation to the groin, traverses the inguinal canal and must be identified during a hernia repair.

Questions

Q223

What is pathognomonic of measles?

*Your Own Answer*_____

Q224

What neoplasm is associated with the most osseous involvement?

*Your Own Answer*_____

Q225

Which enzyme is used by phagocytic cells to disrupt cell walls?

*Your Own Answer*_____

Correct Answers

A223

Koplik's spots are seen in measles (rubeola), which are usually on the buccal mucosa opposite the second molars but can also be found in the conjunctiva, as well as the in the large intestine at autopsy. Koplik's spots are pathognomonic of measles. They are small irregular bright red spots, which usually precede the onset of the exanthem, and in the center of each red spot there is a small bluish-white speck.

A224

Eosinophilic granuloma is a proliferation of Langerhans cells, which is characterized by one or several bone lesions.

A225

Myeloperoxidase uses peroxide to disrupt bacterial cell walls. Deficiency of this enzyme can be associated with recurrent infections.

Questions

Q226

The burning sensation associated with an inflammation of the trachea (tracheitis) would be mediated by what nerve?

*Your Own Answer*_____

Q227

What is the disease that affects predominately young male smokers?

*Your Own Answer*_____

Q228

What are the typical cutaneous manifestations of angioimmunoblastic lymphadenopathy?

*Your Own Answer*_____

Correct Answers

A226

As it ascends in the tracheoesophageal groove, the recurrent laryngeal nerve provides sensory branches to the tracheal mucosa, and thus would mediate a burning sensation.

A227

Thromboangiitis obliterans, or Buerger's disease, affects young to middle-aged male smokers. In contrast, Takayasu's arteritis affects young females in the Orient, and Wegener's granulomatosis occurs in late middle age.

A228

Angioimmunoblastic lymphadenopathy presents with Coomb's-positive hemolytic anemia, rapid onset of fever, lymphadenopathy, and polyclonal hyperglobulinemia. Cutaneous manifestations are usually pruritic macules and papules with some petechiae.

Questions

Q229

A kidney stone lodged in the lower ureter results in pain that is referred where?

*Your Own Answer*_____

Q230

What fungus has the largest spore size?

*Your Own Answer*_____

Q231

Which organism most commonly causes epiglottitis in children?

*Your Own Answer*_____

Correct Answers

A229

The testicles are supplied by sensory nerves that enter the cord at L1 and L2 levels. Sensory nerves supplying the lower ureter also enter the cord at these levels, and this is the basis for the referred pain to the testicles, which is often experienced during the descent of a kidney stone.

A230

Coccidioidomycosis has the largest spore size.

A231

Hemophilus influenzae b causes epiglottitis, which can cause airway compromise in children.

Questions

Q232

A 25-year-old male presents with symptoms of nasal congestion for three weeks, fever, sinus tenderness, and frontal headache. What are the treatment options for this patient's condition?

*Your Own Answer*_____

Q233

Congenital "berry" aneurysms are usually found in which vascular structures?

*Your Own Answer*_____

Q234

What would be completely lacking in the peripheral circulation of an infant born without a thymus?

*Your Own Answer*_____

Correct Answers

A232

This patient has chronic sinusitis. Pneumococcus is the most common organism in sinusitis. Antibiotics are called for. If the disease has an inflammatory component, then nasal steroids such as budesonide, triamcinolone, beconase, and fluticasone are appropriate therapy. Chronic sinusitis unresponsive to all medications for at least one month may require endoscopic sinus surgery. Oral decongestants such as Sudafed are also sometimes helpful.

A233

Congenital "berry" aneurysms are caused by weakened areas that result in saccular enlargements. They occur in the cerebral arteries, including the circle of Willis and the middle cerebral artery.

A234

T-lymphocytes, derived from the thymus, would be lacking.

Questions

Q235

A 40-year-old woman presents with a skin lesion on her upper back. The woman regularly sunbathes. The lesion is raised and has a mottled red, white, and blue appearance. Biopsy shows malignant invasion into the dermis. What is the most likely diagnosis?

*Your Own Answer*_____

Q236

How does histocytic cytophagic panniculitis present?

*Your Own Answer*_____

Q237

The carotid body, located in the vascular wall at the bifurcation of the internal and external carotid arteries, monitors what component of the blood?

*Your Own Answer*_____

Correct Answers

A235

Malignant melanoma is the most likely diagnosis given the history of sunbathing, the appearance of the lesion, and its invasive nature.

A236

Histocytic cytophagic panniculitis is a fatal disease, which presents with painful subcutaneous nodules associated with malaise and fever. It also has hepatosplenomegaly, pancytopenia, and abrupt hemorrhagic death.

A237

The carotid body monitors O_2 and CO_2 and hydrogen ion concentration in the blood. The sensory nerves (branches of cranial nerve IX) supplying the carotid body carry impulses to the respiratory center in the brainstem, and adjustments in the rate of respiration are made accordingly.

Questions

Q238

What is the etiology of Milkers' nodule?

Your Own Answer_____

Q239

What would be destroyed by a skin lesion that results in extensive damage to the dermal papillae in the skin of the fingertips?

Your Own Answer_____

Q240

A 63-year-old man with emphysema and a history of smoking presents with pain, numbness, and weakness of the left arm. Cardiovascular and central nervous system exams are normal. Chest X-ray demonstrates an apical mass on the left lung involving the brachial plexus. What is the most likely diagnosis?

Your Own Answer_____

Correct Answers

A238

Pox virus causes Milker's nodule. Milker's nodule is usually a single, painful nodule on the finger, which is mostly common seen in stockyard and slaughterhouse workers because it is associated with cattle. It also causes skin nodules that are persistent in AIDS patients—not associated with milking.

A239

Meissner's corpuscles are encapsulated tactile receptors located in the dermal papillae, just deep to the stratum basale of the epidermis in areas of hairless skin (palms, fingertips, lips, soles, and nipples). A skin lesion of the fingertips would destroy these corpuscles.

A240

This patient has a classic presentation of a Pancoast tumor. This is an apical tumor that invades the brachial plexus causing neurologic signs in the affected arm.

Questions

Q241

In the inguinal region, the conjoined tendon (falx inguinalis) is formed by a fusion of what?

*Your Own Answer*_____

Q242

Patients with xeroderma pigmentosum are likely to develop skin cancer when exposed to the sun because they have what type of deficiency?

*Your Own Answer*_____

Q243

What is the histologic type of breast cancer characterized by a lymphocytic infiltrate?

*Your Own Answer*_____

Correct Answers

A241

A fusion of the internal oblique and transversus abdominus aponeuroses forms the conjoined tendon.

A242

They have a deficiency of enzymes in the excision repair pathway. Patients with xeroderma pigmentosum have a DNA repair system that does not function properly in the first steps of the excision repair process. They are especially prone to skin cancer because the ultraviolet light, including that from the sun, produces pyrimidine dimers in DNA and since the excision repair pathway has been damaged, DNA cannot be repaired.

A243

Medullary carcinoma is the histologic type of breast cancer that demonstrates a lymphocytic infiltrate. The prognosis for this type is often better than for ductal carcinoma.

Questions

Q244

When a bone is fractured, osteoprogenitor cells undergo intense proliferation around the fracture. These cells are derived from cells in what two structures?

*Your Own Answer*_____

Q245

What are some of the causative agents of granulomatous inflammation?

*Your Own Answer*_____

Q246

What anti-TB agent causes orange urine?

*Your Own Answer*_____

Correct Answers

A244

Osteoprogenitor cells are abundant in the periosteum and endosteum.

A245

M. leprae and *T. pallidium* are bacterial agents, which are associated with the formation of granulomas, as is the fungal infection, cryptococcosis. Surgical suture is a form of a nonimmune foreign body reaction, which is also associated with granulomatous inflammation.

A246

Ethambutol causes orange urine.

Questions

Q247

Compared to capillaries in the rest of the body, capillaries that participate in the formation of the blood-brain barrier have fewer of which structure?

*Your Own Answer*_____

Q248

What is the etiology for typhus?

*Your Own Answer*_____

Q249

A 25-year-old HIV-positive man presents with a new-onset skin lesion. On exam, the lesion is highly vascular. What is the most likely diagnosis?

*Your Own Answer*_____

Correct Answers

A247

Capillaries forming the blood-brain barrier have relatively few pinocytotic vesicles, thus, further limiting movement of substances across the capillary walls.

A248

Rickettsia typhi causes endemic typhus, which is transmitted to humans by rat fleas. *Rickettsia prowazekii* will cause the epidemic typhus, which is transmitted by the human body louse.

A249

Kaposi's sarcoma, a vascular skin tumor, was previously rare. Now, it may be the initial presenting sign of AIDS.

Questions

Q250

The left adrenal vein drains into which vessel?

*Your Own Answer*_____

Q251

A 60-year-old retired salesman is brought to the physician's office by his wife because of progressive dementia, confusion, and memory loss. The geriatrician suspects Alzheimer's disease. What is the treatment for Alzheimer's disease?

*Your Own Answer*_____

Q252

Histologically, how would the thoracic duct differ from the inferior thyroid artery?

*Your Own Answer*_____

Correct Answers

A250

The left adrenal veins drain directly into the left renal vein.

A251

The only approved treatment for the dementia associated with Alzheimer's is the centrally acting cholinesterase inhibitor called tacrine. This drug can cause asymptomatic elevation of liver function tests.

A252

The thoracic duct has valves; the inferior thyroid artery does not.

Questions

Q253

Pellagra can be prevented by ingestion of what vitamin?

*Your Own Answer*_____

Q254

Which oncogene is associated with neuroblastoma?

*Your Own Answer*_____

Q255

In cancer of the prostate gland, metastasis would typically spread to which nodes?

*Your Own Answer*_____

Correct Answers

A253

Pellagra occurs when there is a dietary deficiency of niacin. The symptoms of pellagra include the 3 D's: diarrhea, dementia, and dermatitis. Lack of niacin can also cause a stomatitis.

A254

The myconcogene is associated with neuroblastoma. Oncogenes may be viral (retroviruses) or cellular and cause malignancy by a variety of mechanisms.

A255

Metastasis would spread to the internal iliac nodes, into which the lymphatics of the prostate gland drain.

Questions

Q256

What soft tissue tumor has the worst prognosis?

*Your Own Answer*_____

Q257

The DNA fragment 5'-GAATTC-3' is an example of what kind of sequence?

*Your Own Answer*_____

Q258

What is the function of the Brunner's glands in the duodenum?

*Your Own Answer*_____

Correct Answers

A256

Pleomorphic liposarcoma has a high rate of metastasis and a poorer prognosis than well-differentiated and myxoid liposarcomas.

A257

A palindromic sequence is one that reads the same from 5' to 3' on both strands of the DNA sequence. The opposing strand is formed by using the base pair relationships (G-C, A-T):given 5'-GAATTC-3'opposing 5'-CTTAAG-3'. Since the opposing strand reads the same as the given strand (in the 5' to 3' direction), the sequence is a palindrome.

A258

The submucosal glands of Brunner in the duodenum produce large quantities of alkaline mucus that serves to neutralize gastric juice.

Questions

Q259

What is associated with Romana's sign?

*Your Own Answer*_____

Q260

What is the immune cell found within the early stages of atherosclerotic plaques?

*Your Own Answer*_____

Q261

What antibody class is known to be able to cross the placenta?

*Your Own Answer*_____

Correct Answers

A259

American trypanosomiasis, also known as Chagas' disease, is caused by *Trypanosoma cruzi*. It causes the Romana's sign, which is also known as oculoglandular complex or eye sign—edema and inflammation of the lacrimal glands.

A260

Macrophages are found in the early stages of atherosclerotic plaques known as fatty streaks.

A261

IgG is known to cross the placental barrier, and is thus the most abundant antibody in newborns.

Questions

Q262

What is the most common cause of toxic epidermal necrolysis (TEN) in children?

*Your Own Answer*_____

Q263

In a cross-section of skeletal muscle, the connective tissue forming the perimysium divides the muscle into units. What is the term for these units?

*Your Own Answer*_____

Q264

Human immunodeficiency virus (HIV), the virus causing AIDS, falls into which class?

*Your Own Answer*_____

Correct Answers

A262

Toxic epidermal necrolysis, which is a severe form of Stevens-Johnson syndrome, is a hypersensitivity reaction. Dilantin is the most common cause of TEN in children. Antibiotics, especially the sulfur ones, are the most common causes of TEN in adults.

A263

Surrounded by the perimysium, skeletal muscle fascicles (bundles) are the units of division in the skeletal muscle.

A264

Retroviruses are RNA viruses that use the enzyme reverse transcriptase to make DNA copies of their genome. HIV uses this mechanism to replicate its genome.

Questions

Q265

A 14-year-old girl presents with increased serum bilirubin and vague nonspecific complaints. Laboratory tests show an increase in unconjugated bilirubin with normal liver function tests and negative hepatitis screens. There is no evidence of liver abnormality or of hemolysis. What is the most likely diagnosis?

*Your Own Answer*_____

Q266

A malignant tumor in the lungs has resulted in enlargement of the mediastinal lymph nodes and subsequent compression of the left recurrent laryngeal nerve. This would result in what symptom?

*Your Own Answer*_____

Q267

Prostatic cancer could result in direct lymphogenous spread of tumor cells to which nodes?

*Your Own Answer*_____

Correct Answers

A265

Gilbert's syndrome is a benign condition characterized by an increase in unconjugated bilirubin.

A266

Damage to the recurrent laryngeal nerve unilaterally results in ipsilateral paralysis of the vocal cord and hoarseness.

A267

Lymphatics from the prostate gland drain directly to the internal iliac nodes, and thus, prostatic tumor cells could directly spread to these nodes.

Questions

Q268

A 25-year-old woman visited India on an expedition. Upon returning home, she was found to have a high fever, jaundice, malaise, and anorexia. Her stools were light gray and her urine was amber-colored. Her physician diagnosed her as having hepatitis D (delta-agent). What other form of hepatitis is hepatitis D associated with?

*Your Own Answer*_____

Q269

One of the causes of hemophilia is a deficiency of a protein known as Factor VIII (von Willebrand's factor). This protein is found in granules located in the endothelial cytoplasm of which structure?

*Your Own Answer*_____

Q270

Which group of lymph nodes lie just medial to the femoral vein, and their efferent vessels enter the abdomen by passing though the femoral canal?

*Your Own Answer*_____

Correct Answers

A268

The hepatitis D virus, or delta agent, is a defective RNA virus, which cannot replicate except in the presence of hepatitis B virus. Consequently, it occurs as a co-infection or, in the presence of chronic HBV infections, as a superinfection.

A269

Factor VIII is located in the endothelial cytoplasm of arterioles.

A270

The deep inguinal nodes lie just medial to the femoral vein and send efferent vessels into the abdomen via the femoral canal.

Questions

Q271

What food-borne pathogen may cause splinter hemorrhages on nails?

*Your Own Answer*_____

Q272

A tumor of the parathyroid gland, causing increased blood levels of parathyroid hormone, would increase the activity of which cells?

*Your Own Answer*_____

Q273

A 35-year-old fireman is brought to the emergency room with a burn on his left torso. On examination, the skin of the wound appears charred and no blisters are visible. The man reports no pain when the wound is touched. How would this burn would be classified?

*Your Own Answer*_____

Correct Answers

A271

Splinter hemorrhages are seen in trichinosis, which is caused by *Trichinella spiralis*. The major source of the infection is pork. It usually invades the muscle and sometime the eyes, causing conjunctivitis and periorbital edema. If the parasites invade the nail bed, it causes the splinter hemorrhages.

A272

Osteoclasts and C-cells (parafollicular cells) would exhibit increased activity. Increased blood levels of parathyroid hormone would result in increased bone resorption and mobilization of calcium by osteoclasts. As blood calcium levels rise, the C-cells of the thyroid gland would increase their secretion of calcitonin.

A273

A third-degree burn is one which appears either charred or white and which has no sensation. Burn wounds are classified as either first-, second-, or third-degree. A first-degree burn is characterized by erythema and tenderness to touch. Superficial burns are considered first-degree. A second-degree burn is often characterized by blister formation and is tender on exam.

Questions

Q274

Your patient has a malignant melanoma in the skin, 3 cm directly lateral to the navel. Based on your knowledge of the lymphatic drainage of the area, the most rational course of action would be to surgically remove which lymph nodes?

*Your Own Answer*_____

Q275

In which cell types would you expect to see Birbeck granules?

*Your Own Answer*_____

Q276

Which immunoglobulin is implicated in the development of allergic reactions?

*Your Own Answer*_____

Correct Answers

A274

Since lymphatics on the anterior abdominal wall above the navel drain to the axillary nodes, and those below the navel drain to the superficial inguinal nodes, a cancerous lesion at the level of the navel would indicate removal of both axillary and superficial inguinal nodes.

A275

Birbeck granules are contained in Langerhans' cells, which are antigen-presenting cells located in skin.

A276

IgE is the immunoglobulin implicated in the development of allergic reactions. Binding of antigen by this antibody initiates the process of histamine release.

Questions

Q277

The bronchopulmonary lymph nodes in the inferior lobe of the left lung drain directly to which structure?

*Your Own Answer*_____

Q278

From where do the parathyroid glands receive their blood supply?

*Your Own Answer*_____

Q279

Just proximal to the hilus of the right kidney, the right renal artery passes directly posterior to which structure?

*Your Own Answer*_____

Correct Answers

A277

The nodes in the inferior lobe of the left lung drain directly to the inferior tracheobronchial nodes.

A278

Branches of the superior and inferior thyroid arteries supply the parathyroid glands.

A279

The inferior vena cava crosses directly anterior to the right renal artery.

Questions

Q280

What virus commonly causes retinitis in AIDS patients?

*Your Own Answer*_____

Q281

HLA-B27 is associated with which group of diseases?

*Your Own Answer*_____

Q282

What is the term for the deficiency of vitamin B1 (thiamin)?

*Your Own Answer*_____

Correct Answers

A280

Cytomegalovirus is the virus that causes retinitis in AIDS patients. It can also cause infectious mononucleosis in non-AIDS patients.

A281

HLA-B27 phenotype is associated with autoimmune diseases such as ankylosing spondylitis.

A282

Beriberi is deficiency of vitamin B1 (thiamin). It may manifest itself as peripheral neuropathy or high output heart failure.

Questions

Q283

Just prior to ovulation, the first meiotic division takes place (meiosis I, maturation division). After this division, what is the status of the DNA and how many total chromatids are there?

*Your Own Answer*_____

Q284

What is the inheritance pattern in Wiskott-Aldrich syndrome?

*Your Own Answer*_____

Q285

Bladder cancer is associated with exposure to what type of environmental chemicals?

*Your Own Answer*_____

Correct Answers

A283

Prior to the completion of the first meiotic division, the DNA is 2N, with a total of 46 double-stranded chromosomes. Thus, the first division results in an oocyte containing 23 double-stranded chromosomes (46 chromatids) and DNA.

A284

Wiskott-Aldrich syndrome is inherited in an X-linked manner. Patients with this syndrome present with thrombocytopenia. They also have infections with *Streptococcus pneumonia* or *Hemophilus influenza*. The skin manifestation is similar to atopic dermatitis. They have reduced IgM levels as well as increased IgA and IgE levels.

A285

Aromatic amine exposure has been linked to the development of bladder cancer.

Questions

Q286

What is the anatomical site of the blood-nerve barrier?

*Your Own Answer*_____

Q287

Penicillins affect which cellular function of susceptible bacteria?

*Your Own Answer*_____

Q288

What are the three vascular changes that occur during the early stages of acute inflammation?

*Your Own Answer*_____

Correct Answers

A286

The primary anatomical substrate is the tight junction between endothelial cells of endoneurial capillaries.

A287

Penicillins inhibit cell-wall synthesis and are bactericidal drugs. Sulfa drugs prohibit bacterial folate synthesis. Chloramphenicol, aminoglycosides (e.g., gentamicin), and tetracylines inhibit protein synthesis.

A288

First, there is transient vasoconstriction of the arterioles, leading to decreased blood flow to the injured area. Next, vasodilation causes increased flow of blood to the affected tissue leading to redness and warmth (erythema) of the same area. Finally, stasis is characterized by a slowing of the blood flow and the promotion of margination and emigration of leukocytes, such as neutrophils.

Questions

Q289

What phagocytic cells are members of the mononuclear system?

*Your Own Answer*_____

Q290

What diagnostic test helps to diagnose Sjögren's
syndrome?

*Your Own Answer*_____

Q291

What is associated with the mucosa covering the
inferior nasal concha but not the mucosa in the
olfactory area of the nasal cavity?

*Your Own Answer*_____

Correct Answers

A289

The mono-phagocyte system (MPS) is a collection of phagocytic cells of the bone marrow, peripheral blood, tissues, and the lining of body cavities. Members include macrophages, monocytes, Kupffer cells of the liver, alveolar macrophages of the lung, histiocytes of the connective tissue, osteoclasts of the bone marrow, and microglial cells of the nervous system.

A290

Labial biopsy is the only specific diagnostic technique for Sjögren's syndrome.

A291

Coblet cells are absent in the olfactory epithelium, but are present in the mucosa covering the inferior nasal concha.

Questions

Q292

A newborn infant develops respiratory distress syndrome immediately after birth. X ray demonstrates a severely underdeveloped left lung with loops of bowel in the left chest cavity. What is the most likely diagnosis?

*Your Own Answer*_____

Q293

AIDS is characterized by a deficiency of which type of cell?

*Your Own Answer*_____

Q294

What do watershed infarcts affect?

*Your Own Answer*_____

Correct Answers

A292

Diaphragmatic hernia is a disease of newborns in which abdominal contents spill into the chest cavity through an aperture in the diaphragm, impairing development of the lung. It is much more common on the left than on the right.

A293

CD4+ lymphocytes are T-helper cells, the levels of which drop in AIDS, leaving the patient susceptible to infection.

A294

Watershed infarcts occur in the later phases of shock. They are infarctions in the brains of patients with poor perfusion during shock. Usually, watershed infarcts occur only in patients with pre-existing significant cerebrovascular disease.

Questions

Q295

How is acute disseminated intravascular coagulopathy (DlC) differentiated from chronic DIC?

*Your Own Answer*_____

Q296

A 30-year-old male presents with jaundice, pruritis, and weight loss. On examination, he exhibits signs of cirrhosis and portal hypertension. He denies a history of alcohol ingestion. His past medical history is significant for ulcerative colitis. What is the most likely diagnosis?

*Your Own Answer*_____

Q297

What are the four major side effects of cyclosporine?

*Your Own Answer*_____

Correct Answers

A295

DIC is the formation of platelet-fibrin thrombi in small vessels, principally the arterioles and capillaries, throughout the body. Acute DIC is associated with septic shock and consumption coagulopathy, while chronic DIC is associated with malignancy.

A296

Primary sclerosing cholangitis is associated with ulcerative colitis, and this disease is more common in males. Some patients present with cirrhosis; others with hepatosplenomegaly. The combination of cirrhosis and protal hypertension suggests end-stage disease.

A297

Cyclosporine causes decreased renal function, increased hair growth (hypertrichosis), hyperglycemia, and lipidema. Hypertension, hepatotoxicity, and gingival hyperplasma are other common side effects.

Questions

Q298

Methyl alcohol is metabolized to what substances following ingestion?

*Your Own Answer*_____

Q299

What autoantibodies cause relapsing polychondritis?

*Your Own Answer*_____

Q300

A 36-year-old African-American female presents with anemia and jaundice. Lab tests show hemolysis and a mildly elevated white blood cell count. History is significant because the patient was recently prescribed a sulfa drug for a urinary tract infection. What is the most likely diagnosis?

*Your Own Answer*_____

Correct Answers

A298

Methyl alcohol (methanol) is metabolized to formaldehyde and formic acid. Ingestion of methanol can lead to blindness.

A299

Relapsing polychondritis is a cartilage disease that most commonly involves the ear cartilage as well as the nasal cartilage. It also may present with polyarthritis, ocular inflammation, and respiratory chrondritis. The main problem is autoantibodies to type II collagen.

A300

Glucose-6-phosphate dehydrogenase deficiency is an X-linked condition in which hemolysis occurs in aged red blood cells after exposure to drugs that cause oxidation of hemoglobin and red cell membranes. It is more common in people of African or Mediterranean descent.

Questions

Q301

Topical Ultravate (halobetasol propionate) should not be used where?

*Your Own Answer*_____

Q302

What side effect is commonly related to chloramphenicol administration to neonates?

*Your Own Answer*_____

Q303

Salicylate toxicity typically shows what symptoms?

*Your Own Answer*_____

Correct Answers

A301

Only nonfluorinated topical steroids should be used on the face, and these include hydrocortisone, Westcort, Desowen, etc. However, Ultravate is a fluorinated cortisone cream that is used only two weeks at a time, and it should not be used on the face, intertriginous areas, and axilla since the skin is very thin in those areas.

A302

Gray baby syndrome may be seen when chloramphenicol is administered to neonates. It results from high blood levels due to immature hepatic function and can be fatal.

A303

Tinnitus, deafness, vertigo, and hyperpnea are seen with salycilate intoxication. The hyperpnea may lead to a respiratory alkalosis, but this may be balanced by a metabolic acidosis from the salicylic acid.

Questions

Q304

Chromosome instability syndromes, such as ataxia telangiectasia, Bloom syndrome, Fanconi anemia, and xeroderma pigmentosum share what common characteristics?

*Your Own Answer*_____

Q305

The inheritance of cystic fibrosis is best described by what pattern?

*Your Own Answer*_____

Q306

What is the essential feature of Gardner's syndrome?

*Your Own Answer*_____

Correct Answers

A304

The chromosome instability syndromes are all autosomal recessive traits. They share the characteristics of hypersensitivity to DNA-damaging agents, predisposition to malignancy, deficits of DNA repair or replication and increased chromosome breakages.

A305

Cystic fibrosis follows autosomal recessive inheritance, i.e., a person needs two copies of the gene in order to have the disease.

A306

Gardner's syndrome is an autosomal dominant syndrome, which manifests with multiple epidermoid cysts, especially in the jaw area, as well as osteomas of the facial bones. It also causes intestinal polyposis. Fibromas, desmoids, and other lipomas are also characteristics of this syndrome.

Questions

Q307

A 30-year-old Type I (juvenile) diabetic male is brought to the emergency room in a coma. Laboratory studies demonstrate hyperglycemia and hyperketonemia. What other metabolic derangement might be expected?

*Your Own Answer*_____

Q308

What class of drugs is used to treat tinea versicolor?

*Your Own Answer*_____

Q309

In proteins, the a-helix and b-pleated sheet are examples of what type of structure?

*Your Own Answer*_____

Correct Answers

A307

This patient clearly has diabetic ketoacidosis. This condition is characterized by metabolic acidosis.

A308

Tinea versicolor is treated with anti-fungal agents.

A309

The a-helix and b-pleated sheet are examples of secondary structure. Secondary structure refers to the steric interaction between amino acids situated next to each other.

Questions

Q310

A 53-year-old male presents to an emergency room at 2:00 a.m. with excruciating pain of his left great toe. His history is significant for moderate alcohol intake and a fatty meal earlier in the evening. There is no history of trauma. One might expect to find deposition of which substance in the joint space?

*Your Own Answer*_____

Q311

The thoracolumbar fascia of the back is continuous laterally with what portion of the abdominal wall?

*Your Own Answer*_____

Q312

What neoplasm presents similarly to Mondor's disease?

*Your Own Answer*_____

Correct Answers

A310

This patient presents with the typical history for an attack of gout. If fluid were aspirated from the joint space, urate crystals would be found.

A311

Scarpa's fascia of the anterior abdominal wall attaches to the thoracolumbar fascia in the back.

A312

Mondor's disease is thrombophlebitis of the anterior chest wall. It can present itself as a tender or nontender chord, and it is often confused with breast cancer.

Questions

Q313

In mammals, which amino acid is not essential because it can be synthesized from phenylalanine?

*Your Own Answer*_____

Q314

Damage to which structure would result in denervation of the detrusor muscle, and severely hinder emptying of the bladder?

*Your Own Answer*_____

Q315

What disease is associated with Woronoff ring?

*Your Own Answer*_____

Correct Answers

A313

Tyrosine is not essential because it can be synthesized directly from phenylalanine. The reaction is catalyzed by phenylalanine hydroxylase.

A314

Damage to the pelvic splanchnic nerves, which supply the parasympathetic innervation to the smooth muscle of the bladder, would result in denervation of the detrusor muscle.

A315

Woronoff ring is a hyperpigmentation around the psoriatic plaque, which is due to prostaglandins.

Questions

Q316

What is the carcinogen that can be found in association with peanuts?

*Your Own Answer*_____

Q317

What is an example of an autosomal-recessive disorder that leads to an increased risk of cancer?

*Your Own Answer*_____

Q318

What is the drug treatment of choice for metastatic colon cancer?

*Your Own Answer*_____

Correct Answers

A316

Aflatoxin may be found in peanuts and is associated with hepatic cancer.

A317

Ataxia-telangiectasia is an autosomal-recessive disorder that is characterized by a defect in a protein that stops the cell cycle in response to cell damage. This leads to chromosomal instability and increased sensitivity to killing by X-irradiation or gamma-irradiation, increasing the risk of cancer.

A318

5-fluorouracil is a chemotherapeutic agent that has been used to treat metastatic colon carcinoma for over 30 years. It can be given by the intravenous route, arterial infusion, intraperitoneally, or orally. Its side effects include leukopenia, diarrhea, stomatitis, and intractable vomiting. 5-fluorouracil is commonly given in combination with levamisole, an immune system stimulator, and leucovorin (folinic acid).

Questions

Q319

In premature newborns, respiratory distress syndrome may result from the large number of which immature, non-functional cells?

*Your Own Answer*_____

Q320

In a histological section of the superficial fascia (hypodermis) from the abdominal wall of an average 38-year-old male, what type of tissue would predominate?

*Your Own Answer*_____

Q321

In a patient with Horner's syndrome, what would be the status of arterioles associated with arteriovenous anastomoses in the skin of the face?

*Your Own Answer*_____

Correct Answers

A319

Type II (great) alveolar cells produce surfactant, and their immaturity in premature infants directly relates to respiratory distress syndrome.

A320

Adipose tissue and loose connective tissue predominate in the superficial fascia.

A321

In Horner's syndrome, resulting from a lesion of the sympathetic trunk, the arterioles in the skin, including those of AV anastomoses, would dilate, leading to the characteristic flushing and warmness of the skin of the face.

Questions

Q322

What is Osler-Weber-Rendu disease?

*Your Own Answer*_____

Q323

Azelaic acid inhibits what enzyme?

*Your Own Answer*_____

Q324

How can bezoars be treated?

*Your Own Answer*_____

Correct Answers

A322

Osler-Weber-Rendu disease is an autosomal dominant hemorrhagic telangiectasia, which involves the skin, mucosal surfaces, and internal organs. It is not a congenital disorder, though it is a hereditary disorder.

A323

Azelaic acid is actually secreted by pitryosporum orbiculare (Malassezia furfur), which is the etiology of tinea versicolor, and that inhibits tyrosinase, which is the rate-limiting step in melanin production.

A324

Bezoars are non-digestable items found in the stomach, frequently made of hair (trichobezoar). They may be treated with papain, acetylcysteine, or cellulase (for phytobezoar). Surgery may also be indicated.

Questions

Q325

What bacterial species is implicated in the development of duodenal ulcers?

*Your Own Answer*_____

Q326

What antibody class is involved in the primary response to an antigen?

*Your Own Answer*_____

Q327

A bacterium entering a lymph node via an afferent lymph vessel would initially traverse which structure in the lymph node?

*Your Own Answer*_____

Correct Answers

A325

Helicobacter pylori is implicated in the development of gastric and duodenal ulcers.

A326

IgM, a pentamer, is the main antibody produced in the primary response to an antigen. It is the most efficient in complement fixation and agglutination.

A327

The afferent lymph vessels drain directly into the subcapsular sinus upon reaching the node.

Questions

Q328

What causes erythrasma?

*Your Own Answer*_____

Q329

What drug is associated with the development of Reye's syndrome in children?

*Your Own Answer*_____

Q330

A patient presents with drooping of the upper eyelid, a constricted pupil, and dryness and flushing of the skin of the face. The symptoms are all unilateral. What structure is likely damaged?

*Your Own Answer*_____

Correct Answers

A328

Corynebacterium minutissumum will cause erythrasma.

A329

Reye's syndrome is an encepholapathic syndrome seen in children with acute viral infections who are administered aspirin.

A330

The symptoms listed (ptosis, miosis, anhydrosis, flushing) are diagnostic for Horner's syndrome, resulting from a lesion of some portion of the sympathetic pathway, usually the sympathetic trunk.

Questions

Q331

Where are atherosclerotic lesions of arteries initiated?

*Your Own Answer*_____

Q332

What is the major component of amyloid?

*Your Own Answer*_____

Q333

What are four causes of Reynaud's phenomenon?

*Your Own Answer*_____

Correct Answers

A331

The tunica intima, particularly the endothelium, is the site of initial pathology in atherosclerotic lesions of blood vessels.

A332

Protein fibrils that are derived from normal, soluble proteins make up close to 85-95% of amyloid. P component and proteoglycans are the other components of amyloid. Amyloid is an abnormal, insoluble material that is deposited in various tissues and organs in a group of very heterogeneous diseases.

A333

Collagen vascular disease, obstructive arterial disease, neurological disorders (such as carpal tunnel syndrome), multiple sclerosis, drugs (such as beta adrenergic blockers), may cause Raynaud's phenomenon. Hyperthyroidism, cryoproteins, and polycythemia may also cause Raynaud's phenomenon. Patients who work with vibratory tools, meat cutters, pianists, and typists may also present with Raynaud's phenomenon.

Questions

Q334

With what inflammatory disease do a large proportion of patients develop secondary amyloidosis?

*Your Own Answer*_____

Q335

A 13-year old girl has sulfur-deficient brittle hair and is mentally and physically retarded. She is found to be extremely sensitive to UV radiation. What is the most likely diagnosis?

*Your Own Answer*_____

Q336

Following a myocardial infarction, what happens to cardiac muscle?

*Your Own Answer*_____

Correct Answers

A334

15-25% of patients with rheumatoid arthritis develop secondary amyloidosis.

A335

Trichothiodystrophy (PIBIDS) is characterized by sulfur-deficient brittle hair and mental and physical retardation. It is caused by a defect in transcription complex proteins, such as RNA polymerase II, which is involved in nucleotide excision repair. The deficiency leads to increased cellular sensitivity to killing by UV radiation.

A336

Since cardiac muscle does not have the regenerative capacity of skeletal muscle, a myocardial infarction results in degeneration of muscle fibers, followed by scarring of the area of the infarct.

Questions

Q337

Which syndrome is associated with adrenal cortical hemorrhage, septic shock, necrosis, and neisseria meningitidis?

*Your Own Answer*_____

Q338

Your patient has a tumor (1 cm diameter) in the posterior mediastinum, just posterior to the left atrium of the heart, which is compressing the anterior surface of the esophagus. What other structure is most likely to be damaged in this situation?

*Your Own Answer*_____

Q339

How is the microanatomy of veins and lymphatic vessels similar?

*Your Own Answer*_____

Correct Answers

A337

Waterhouse-Friderichsen syndrome is a hemorrhagic necrosis of the cortex of the adrenal glands, which occurs in cases of septic shock. It is usually caused by *Neisseria meningitidis* and is usually seen in children.

A338

The left vagus nerve would likely be damaged as it assumes an anterior position along the esophagus in the mediastinum.

A339

Most veins (other than emissary veins) and lymphatic vessels have valves to prevent backflow.

Questions

Q340

What symptoms are typically seen in Kawasaki disease?

*Your Own Answer*_____

Q341

What is the causative organism of Hansen's disease?

*Your Own Answer*_____

Q342

What effect do insulinoma, glucose-6-phosphatase deficiency, Addison's disease, and insulin injections have on blood glucose levels?

*Your Own Answer*_____

Correct Answers

A340

Kawasaki disease is mostly seen in children. It has multiple components including fever for at least five days and conjunctival injection, erythema and swelling of both palms, soles, and lips, a polymorphous exanthem of the skin, and lymph node enlargement. Strawberry tongue is also seen in Kawasaki disease.

A341

Hansen's disease, also known as leprosy, is caused by *Mycobacterium leprae*. This organism causes a spectrum of diseases, including massive loss of tissue in its most severe forms.

A342

An excess of insulin (via insulinoma or insulin injection) can produce hypoglycemia or decreased blood glucose levels. G6PD deficiency causes hypoglycemia because gluconeogenesis is inhibited. Addison's disease produces hypoglycemia because of a lack of glucocorticoids.

Questions

Q343

Duchenne muscular dystrophy is transmitted according to which genetic pattern?

*Your Own Answer*_____

Q344

In allergic hypersensitivity reactions in the skin, what releases histamine?

*Your Own Answer*_____

Q345

When doing a mediolateral episiotomy during childbirth, the skin, posterolateral wall of the vagina, and what other structure are cut?

*Your Own Answer*_____

Correct Answers

A343

Duchenne muscular dystrophy is transmitted in X-linked fashion. Patients present with proximal muscle weakness.

A344

Mast cells produce histamine, which causes vasodilation and leakage of fluid from capillaries and venules into the intercellular space.

A345

The bulbospongiosus muscle, closely apposed to the vaginal wall, typically is severed during an episiotomy.

Questions

Q346

An increased risk of hepatic tumors, deep venous thromboses (DVTs), myocardial infarction, and pulmonary infarction is associated with which drug?

*Your Own Answer*_____

Q347

What are the 5 "P's" of lichen planus?

*Your Own Answer*_____

Q348

True or False: Females have a greater risk of developing invasive cancer than do males.

*Your Own Answer*_____

Correct Answers

A346

Oral contraceptive pills (OCPs) increase the risk of hepatic tumors, DVTs, heart disease leading to myocardial infarction, and pulmonary infarction from pulmonary emboli. In other words, OCPs create a hypercoagulable state.

A347

Lichen planus is a skin condition, which is very pruritic and manifests itself as violaceous purple, planar, and polygonal papules on the flexural surfaces. Therefore it is known as the five P's, *p*ruritic, *p*urple, *p*lanar, *p*olygonal, *p*apular. Lichen planus can also manifest on mucosal surfaces, such as on the genitalia and oral mucosa, and these might become very painful and ulcerative. There is no good treatment.

A348

False. Males have a greater lifetime risk of developing invasive cancer than do females.

Questions

Q349

The diseases shingles, chickenpox (varicella), cytomegalic inclusion disease, and mononucleosis are all caused by what group of viruses?

*Your Own Answer*_____

Q350

What is the leading site of origin of fatal cancers in females?

*Your Own Answer*_____

Q351

In cancer of the parotid gland, metastasis of tumor cells from the gland would initially spread to what nodes?

*Your Own Answer*_____

Correct Answers

A349

The herpesviruses include herpes simplex virus (HSV), varicella-zoster virus (VZV), cytomegalic virus (CMV), and Epstein-Barr virus (EBV). VZV causes shingles and chickenpox, CMV causes cellular inclusions, and EBV causes infectious mononucleosis.

A350

Cancer originating in the lung is responsible for 25% of fatal cancers in females. Cancer originating in the breast is responsible for 17%, colon and rectum for 10%, lymphoma and leukemia for 8%, ovary for 6%, pancreas for 5%, urinary tract for 3%, uterus for 2%, and uterine cervix for 2%.

A351

The metastasis would spread to the deep cervical nodes, into which the parotid nodes drain.

Questions

Q352

When doing surgery on the thyroid gland, the arteries and veins of the gland must be identified and ligated. Which vessel runs posterior to the carotid sheath and sympathetic trunk prior to reaching the gland?

*Your Own Answer*_____

Q353

In which layer of the skin does the bullae form in pemphigus vulgaris?

*Your Own Answer*_____

Q354

What is the most common manifestation of SLE?

*Your Own Answer*_____

Correct Answers

A352

The inferior thyroid artery enters the gland after passing posterior to the carotid sheath.

A353

Pemphigus vulgaris is one of the primary bullous diseases of the skin. The blister formation occurs within the epidermis.

A354

Arthritis is a common manifestation of lupus. However, patients also have skin findings in addition to photosensitivity, pleuritis, nephritis, oral lesions, and neurologic and hematologic abnormalities.

Questions

Q355

Pemphigus vulgaris usually has its first manifestations on which body part?

*Your Own Answer*_____

Q356

A 32-year-old male of Middle Eastern origin presented with uveitis, genital ulcers, and recurrent oral ulcers. He also complained of joint pain in the knees and ankles. Lab tests were positive for HLA-B51. What is the most likely diagnosis?

*Your Own Answer*_____

Q357

How does the microanatomy of a medium vein differ from a medium artery?

*Your Own Answer*_____

Correct Answers

A355

The mouth

A356

Behcet's disease is a multisystem syndrome associated with uveitis, genital and oral ulcers, and phlebitis and arthritis of the knees. It occurs most frequently in the Mediterranean, the Middle East, and Japan, affecting men significantly more often than women.

A357

Medium veins characteristically have a lumen with fewer layers of smooth muscle than a comparable medium artery.

Questions

Q358

The influx of what ion is normally seen with cell death due to ischemia?

*Your Own Answer*_____

Q359

Beriberi is caused by a deficiency of which vitamin?

*Your Own Answer*_____

Q360

In the epidermis, what would be affected by a defect in the metabolism of tyrosine?

*Your Own Answer*_____

Correct Answers

A358

There is a large calcium influx upon cell death.

A359

Thiamine deficiency causes beriberi. There are two types of beriberi, "wet" and "dry." "Wet beriberi causes high-output congestive heart failure. "Dry" beriberi is associated with neurological symptoms.

A360

The formation of melanin would be affected because tyrosine is a key precursor in the synthesis of melanin by melanocytes.

Questions

Q361

A 56-year-old alcoholic man comes into the emergency room vomiting blood. History is significant for a prolonged episode of vomiting. Endoscopy demonstrates a lateral tear of the stomach at the level of the gastroesophageal junction. What is the most likely diagnosis?

*Your Own Answer*_____

Q362

Blunt trauma in the back that fractures the right 12th rib would likely damage (bruise) which structure?

*Your Own Answer*_____

Q363

A 36-year-old male presents with sudden onset of severe left toe pain. He was found to have hyperuricemia. Negatively birefringent crystals were seen on the polarized light microscope after aspiration of the crystals from the first left metatarsophalangeal joint. The physician prescribed colchicine for this acute episode of gouty arthritis. What are some side effects of colchicine?

*Your Own Answer*_____

Correct Answers

A361

Mallory-Weiss syndrome describes a tear in the stomach at the level of the gastroesophageal junction, usually preceded by prolonged vomiting.

A362

The right kidney is crossed diagonally by the 12th rib and would likely be vulnerable to this type of injury.

A363

Diarrhea is a very common side effect of colchicine given by the oral route. Nausea and vomiting are also common side effects. Abdominal pain is usually the presenting side effect of colchicine used to treat gouty arthritis. Hemorrhagic gastroenteritis is a rare toxicity in long-term or high-dose colchicine administration. Aplastic anemia, thrombocytopenia, and agranulocytosis are some of the hematologic side effects of long-term colchicine administration.

Questions

Q364

A compromised blood flow in the left gastric artery would lead to ischemia of which structure?

*Your Own Answer*_____

Q365

The ovarian arteries reach the ovary via the suspensory ligaments of the ovary. These are also known by what term?

*Your Own Answer*_____

Q366

White forelock is associated with what autosomal dominant neurological disease?

*Your Own Answer*_____

Correct Answers

A364

Ischemia of the lower esophagus would result, since the lower esophagus receives its blood supply from esophageal branches of the left gastric artery.

A365

The suspensory ligament of the ovary is often referred to clinically as the infundibulopelvic ligament.

A366

White forelock is associated with Waardenburg-Klein syndrome. This is autosomal dominant. The inner canthis of the eyes are displaced laterally. The irises are heterochromic and sometimes may lack pigmentation. Piebaldness with deafness and partial albinism are all part of the syndrome.

Questions

Q367

Lymphogenous spread of tumor cells from a cancerous ovary would initially spread to which nodes?

*Your Own Answer*_____

Q368

Why is sodium nitrite used to treat cyanide poisoning?

*Your Own Answer*_____

Q369

A lipid-rich watery fluid is found to be accumulating in the posterior mediastinum of a patient following surgery to remove metastatic tumors from a lung cancer. This occurrence suggests damage to what structure?

*Your Own Answer*_____

Correct Answers

A367

The lymphatics from the ovaries drain directly to the para-aortic (lateral aortic and pre-aortic) nodes, and thus, ovarian tumor cells would initially spread to these nodes.

A368

Sodium nitrite is used as treatment because it oxidizes hemoglobin to methemoglobin. Methemoglobin competes with cytochrome oxidase for cyanide, and, thus, oxidative phosphorylation may resume.

A369

The thoracic duct carries a lipid-rich watery fluid and is located within the posterior mediastinum. It is vulnerable in this surgical procedure.

Questions

Q370

Obstruction of the duct of a sebaceous gland often results in a sebaceous cyst. The substance that accumulates in the cyst would be rich in what compound?

*Your Own Answer*_____

Q371

A 2-month-old infant is brought to the physician's office by her mother because of a fever of 104° and lethargy. The pediatrician strongly suspects meningitis, and performs a lumbar puncture. The CSF contains elevated WBC levels. Cultures are pending. What organisms should be suspected?

*Your Own Answer*_____

Q372

What is directly related to lung compliance?

*Your Own Answer*_____

Correct Answers

A370

Sebum, the substance that is produced by sebaceous glands and accumulates in the cyst, is rich in lipids.

A371

H. influenzae is responsible for most cases of meningitis in children greater than 1 month of age. *N. meningitidis* is a Gram-negative diplococci, which is a cause of meningitis most often in the first year of life.

A372

Elastic fibers in the alveolar wall are directly related to the property of lung compliance.

Questions

Q373

What is the most common form of hypertension?

*Your Own Answer*_____

Q374

A gunshot wound has damaged the diaphragm and the diaphragmatic surface of the heart. What structure of the heart was most likely damaged because of its contact relationship with the diaphragm?

*Your Own Answer*_____

Q375

What is Mohs surgery used to treat?

*Your Own Answer*_____

Correct Answers

A373

Essential, or "idiopathic," hypertension causes 90-95% of all cases of hypertension. Essential hypertension may be benign or malignant. Benign forms account for 95% and malignant forms for 5% of all cases of essential hypertension. The other 5% are secondary to endocrine, renovascular, renal, neurogenic, or iatrogenic disorders.

A374

The left ventricle lies in direct contact with the diaphragm and was most likely damaged.

A375

Mohs surgery is a special way of treating skin cancer. Mohs surgery is not only the surgeon, but also the pathologist who excises the tissue in horizontal layers and examines it under the microscope at the same time for complete removal of the tumor.

Questions

Q376

The pain from inflammation of the costal pleurae at the level of the 3rd, 4th, and 5th ribs would be referred to which structure?

*Your Own Answer*_____

Q377

What are three cutaneous manifestations of Sjögren's syndrome?

*Your Own Answer*_____

Q378

What is the most common location for chondrodermatitis nodularis helicis?

*Your Own Answer*_____

Correct Answers

A376

The costal pleura is supplied by intercostal nerves, thus, pain originating in the costal pleura superiorly would be referred to the upper portion of the thoracic wall.

A377

Cutaneous manifestations of Sjögren's syndrome include keratoconjunctivitis sicca, xerostomia, nasal dryness, vaginal dryness, dry skin, hyper- and hypopigmentation, patch alopecia, Raynaud's phenomenon, vasculitis, and cryoglobulinemia.

A378

Chondrodermatitis nodularis helicis (Winkler's disease) is a cartilage problem, which presents as a painful nodule, most commonly on the helix of the ear, however, it is seen in other places on the ear.

Questions

Q379

What causes river blindness?

*Your Own Answer*_____

Q380

What type of chromosome abnormality is most frequent in unselected spontaneous abortions?

*Your Own Answer*_____

Q381

What organ is predominantly involved in the acute-phase reaction?

*Your Own Answer*_____

Correct Answers

A379

Onchocerciasis is caused by *Onchocera volvulus*, which is commonly found in Africa and Central America. The vector is the black fly and it affects the connective tissue and lymphatics of the skin and sometimes the eye. It causes keratitis, iritis, and choroiditis, which leads to blindness. The most characteristic skin manifestation is a painless mobile subcutaneous nodule around the adult worm.

A380

Autosomal trisomy accounts for 52% of all chromosomal abnormalities found in unselected spontaneous abortions. 45, X accounts for 19%, triploidy for 16%, tetraploidy for 5.5%, and others for 7%.

A381

Albumin accounts for about 60% of the protein in plasma. It is synthesized by the liver. The liver also synthesizes most of the other plasma proteins, and thus is the most important organ in the acute phase reaction.

Questions

Q382

Which three drugs may result in the production of anti-histone antibodies?

*Your Own Answer*_____

_____

Q383

What is nevoid basal cell carcinoma syndrome?

*Your Own Answer*_____

_____

Q384

A thrombosis of a branch of the middle cerebral artery has resulted in extensive damage to the precentral gyrus. What would be the result?

*Your Own Answer*_____

_____

Correct Answers

A382

Procainamide, Hydralazine, and Dilantin may cause anti-histone antibodies.

A383

Nevoid basal cell carcinoma syndrome is an inherited disease with multiple basal cells, as well as jaw cysts and nervous system tumors. The most common malignant tumor that is associated with nevoid basal cell carcinoma syndrome is medulloblastoma.

A384

Damage to the precentral gyrus, the site of primary motor cortex, would result in contralateral upper motor neuron signs.

Questions

Q385

A tumor lying directly on the anterior surface of the anterior scalene muscle could result in respiratory distress due to compression of the which structure?

*Your Own Answer*_____

Q386

A patient presents with postprandial fullness and a history of neurosis. X-ray demonstrates a mass in the gastric lumen. An endoscopic biopsy is taken that is positive for hair. What is the most likely diagnosis?

*Your Own Answer*_____

Q387

Suppose a patient makes autoantibodies against his own red blood cells. Which cells of the immune system are likely to be deficient?

*Your Own Answer*_____

Correct Answers

A385

Respiratory distress could result from compression of the phrenic nerve, which descends along the anterior surface of the anterior scalene muscle and supplies motor innervation to the diaphragm.

A386

Bezoars are accumulations of retained substances in the stomach; a trichobezoar is made of hair swallowed by the patient, often by neurotic habit.

A387

Suppressor T-cells may suppress B-cell responses to antigens, thus preventing antibody synthesis. Lack of suppressor T-cells may thus allow the existence of B-cells that recognize self-antigens and thus are able to produce auto-antibodies.

Questions

Q388

How does dermatomyositis present?

*Your Own Answer*_____

Q389

Organisms that lack both superoxide dismutase and catalase are known by what term?

*Your Own Answer*_____

Q390

In a histological section of the lungs, how would a segmental (tertiary) bronchus differ from a bronchiole?

*Your Own Answer*_____

Correct Answers

A388

Dermatomyositis is a muscle disorder, which presents itself with weakness of the proximal muscles as well as some cutaneous findings, such as periorbital erythema, which is known as heliotrope. Patients also have papules on their knuckles, elbows, and knees, which are called the Grottron papules. All the enzymes that are produced by the muscles, such as CPK, aldolase, and LDH, will be abnormal in dermatomyositis.

A389

Organisms that lack superoxide dismutase and catalase lack the ability to detoxify O_2 radicals and hydrogen peroxide, respectively. These two molecules are toxic to the cell and, thus, the organisms (e.g., *Clostridium tetani*) cannot live in the presence of oxygen and are known as obligate anaerobes.

A390

The bronchiole would have no cartilage in its wall.

Questions

Q391

What syndrome is associated with recurrent "cold" staphylococcal abscesses?

*Your Own Answer*_____

Q392

A 26-year-old woman is stung by a bee. Within a few minutes, she faints. Her pulse is barely palpable and she appears pale. What is the most likely diagnosis?

*Your Own Answer*_____

Q393

A 17-year-old African-American woman presents with severe abdominal pain. Lab studies show anemia with abnormal hemoglobin electrophoresis 3/4 significant for the presence of hemoglobin S. What is the most likely cause of the woman's symptoms and lab abnormalities?

*Your Own Answer*_____

Correct Answers

A391

Job's syndrome is also known as hyperimmuno-globulinemia E recurrent infectious syndrome. Patients have recurrent infections, cold staphylococcal abscesses, and increased immunoglobulin E levels, which are usually more than 1,000 international units. It is usually seen in patients with fair skin and in red-headed girls.

A392

Type I hypersensitivity reactions refer to allergic or anaphylactic reactions. In this case, allergy to bee sting caused anaphylaxis.

A393

The presentation of abdominal pain and hemo-globin S in an African-American suggests sickle cell disease. The abnormal red blood cells cause microvascular occlusion since they do not pass normally through blood vessels; this leads to pain.

Questions

Q394

What are the three general stages of shock?

*Your Own Answer*_____

Q395

What malignancy is commonly associated with in utero exposure to diethylstilbestrol (DES)?

*Your Own Answer*_____

Q396

A 32-year-old female complaining of fever, weight loss, night sweats, and pruritis was found on examination to have diffuse lymphadenopathy. Chest X ray revealed mediastinal adenopathy. Her physician diagnosed her as having nodular sclerosing Hodgkin's disease after performing a bone marrow biopsy. What bone marrow finding is diagnostic of Hodgkins's disease?

*Your Own Answer*_____

Correct Answers

The first, or nonprogressive phase, is characterized **A394** by an increase in cardiac output and peripheral vaso- constriction. There is no tissue injury, but there is an increase in sympathetic activity as the neurohumoral reflexes take over. During the progressive phase, there is reversible tissue injury, lactic acidosis due to anaerobic metabolism, periph- eral vasodilation, and stasis of blood in the periphery, re- ducing cardiac output. The irreversible phase is character- ized by death resulting from multiple organ failure (usually renal failure).

A395

Clear cell adenocarcinoma of the vagina and cervix is the particular histologic malignancy seen in patients with in utero exposure to DES.

A396

Reed-Sternberg cells found in the bone marrow are large, bilobed cells with prominent eosinophilic nucleoli, thick nuclear membrane, and a relatively abundant cytoplasm. A stromal background is re- quired for the Reed-Sternberg cell in order to make the histological diagnosis of Hodgkins's disease.

Questions

Q397

A 67-year-old male wakes up in the middle of the night complaining of severe shortness of breath. He was brought to the emergency room and was found to have rales on lung auscultation, pedal edema, elevation of jugular veins, and tachycardia. The physician diagnosed congestive heart failure. What tests are useful to diagnose systolic dysfunction of the ventricle?

*Your Own Answer*_____

Q398

A 40-year-old female reports feelings of panic when she leaves her house and goes to a public place. She increasingly stays home to avoid these feelings. What is she most likely suffering from?

*Your Own Answer*_____

Q399

A 63-year-old man presents with a heart murmur and is found to have a valvular abnormality. History is significant for a severe infectious illness with arthritis during childhood. At surgery, the valve is found to be severely calcified. What is the most likely cause of the valvular abnormality?

*Your Own Answer*_____

Correct Answers

A397

A chest X ray would reveal the consequences of systolic dysfunction. Exercise stress testing would reveal significant left ventricular dysfunction. An echocardiogram would reveal a left ventricular ejection fraction less than 50%. MUGA scan is a nuclear medicine test that offers rapid and efficient imaging of the left ventricle during rest and exercise.

A398

Agoraphobia (the fear of being in a public place)

A399

Group A Streptococcus causes rheumatic fever, which can lead to heart valve abnormalities later in life.

Questions

Q400

A fracture of the left 11th rib could possibly result in damage to which structure?

*Your Own Answer*_____

Q401

What are the common features of Gram-positive bacteria?

*Your Own Answer*_____

Q402

What is a common side effect of Dapsone?

*Your Own Answer*_____

Correct Answers

A400

The left kidney rests higher along the posterior abdominal wall, directly related to the 11th and 12th ribs, and would be vulnerable to injury by a fracture of the 11th rib.

A401

Gram-positive bacteria stain blue after Gram stain and have a thicker peptidoglycan layer than Gram-negative bacteria. Teichoic acids are found on Gram-positive bacteria, and may be antigenic. Streptococci and staphylococci are common examples of Gram-positive bacteria.

A402

Blue lips are caused by methemoglobinemia, which is a serious side effect of Dapsone.

Questions

Q403

A four-year-old female presents with abdominal pain, palpable abdominal mass, and hematuria. Radiologic studies demonstrate a solid mass in the right kidney. What is the most likely diagnosis?

*Your Own Answer*_____

Q404

What antibody class is involved in anaphylactic reactions?

*Your Own Answer*_____

Q405

The nucleus gracilis and nucleus cuneatus in the medulla receive their input from fibers that form which structure?

*Your Own Answer*_____

Correct Answers

A403

Wilms' tumor usually presents with abdominal pain, mass, and hematuria. It is the most common renal malignancy of early childhood.

A404

The Fc region of the IgE immunoglobulin binds to basophils and mast cells. If an antigen (e.g., bee venom) then binds to this IgE-cell complex, an anaphylactic reaction is triggered to the release of various mediators (e.g., histamine).

A405

The majority of the fibers of the dorsal columns of the spinal cord synapse in the nucleus gracilis and nucleus cuneatus (dorsal column nuclei) in the caudal medulla.

Questions

Q406

A 46-year-old woman complains of severe pruritis over several months. On examination, she is found to have hepatomegaly, and lab data reveal elevated serum alkaline phosphatase, serum cholesterol, and anti-mitochondrial antibody titers. What is the most likely diagnosis?

*Your Own Answer*_____

Q407

A 19-year-old male presents with complaints of lack of sexual desire, decreased libido, decreased facial and body hair and poor muscle strength. His physician diagnosed primary hypogonadism. What are clinical characteristics of primary hypogonadism?

*Your Own Answer*_____

Q408

What is the normal position of the uterus in the pelvic cavity?

*Your Own Answer*_____

Correct Answers

A406

Primary biliary cirrhosis is common in middle-aged women. It is associated with jaundice, hepatosplenomegaly and xanthomata. Portal hypertension is present in late-stage disease. Alkaline phosphatase levels are usually elevated.

A407

Serum LH and FSH levels are elevated in primary hypogonadism because of the lack of testosterone production in the gonads. Serum testosterone levels are low secondary to decreased production in the scrotum. Lack of testosterone can lead to decreases in erythropoiesis, osteoporosis, and decreases in muscle mass. Life-long androgen replacement in the form of intramuscular testosterone and transdermal testosterone patches are needed in primary hypogonadism.

A408

The uterus may assume a variety of positions under various conditions, but normally it is anteverted and anteflexed.

Questions

Q409

What fungus has the smallest spore size?

*Your Own Answer*_____

Q410

During surgical repair of a hernia, the genital branch of the genitofemoral nerve was accidentally cut, resulting in denervation of which muscle?

*Your Own Answer*_____

Q411

Treatment with digoxin might affect the blood levels of what commonly used drug involved in the coagulation pathway?

*Your Own Answer*_____

Correct Answers

A409

Histoplamosis has the smallest spore size.

A410

The cremaster muscle is innervated by the genital branch of the genitofemoral nerve.

A411

Both digoxin and warfarin are metabolized by the hepatic cytochrome P450 system, and so interact with each other.

Questions

Q412

What is the mechanism of action of methotrexate?

*Your Own Answer*_____

Q413

SAA (serum amyloid A) protein, C-reactive protein, haptoglobin, and fibrinogen are all examples of which acute-phase reactants?

*Your Own Answer*_____

Q414

The pathologic lesions in Henoch-Schönlein purpura would demonstrate deposition of which substance?

*Your Own Answer*_____

Correct Answers

A412

Methotrexate is a folic acid analog and it inhibits the dihydrofolate reductase enzyme, which is required in DNA synthesis.

A413

SAA protein, C-reactive protein, haptoglobin, and fibrinogen are all positive acute-phase reactants. Negative acute-phase reactants include transferrin, albumin, and transthyretin.

A414

Henoch-Schönlein purpura is hemorrhagic urticaria with renal involvement. The renal lesions demonstrate deposition of IgA.

Questions

Q415

In long bones, what process initially forms the compact bone in the bone collar of the shaft?

*Your Own Answer*_____

Q416

With what disease is paraprotein most closely associated?

*Your Own Answer*_____

Q417

What is the primary indicated use of dapsone?

*Your Own Answer*_____

Correct Answers

A415

The initial formation of the bone collar is by intramembranous ossification.

A416

Paraprotein is an abnormal monoclonal immunoglobulin or free light chain, which is detectable in the serum of most patients with AL amyloid. It is seen in persons with multiple myeloma or benign monoclonal gammopathy.

A417

Dapsone is the indicated treatment for leprosy.

Questions

Q418

A 60-year-old male complains of weakness, fatigue, and bleeding from the oronasal area. He also has blurred vision, dyspnea, and pallor. Physical exam shows lymphadenopathy, hepatosplenomegaly, and sensorimotor peripheral neuropathy. Bone marrow aspirate revealed hypercellular infiltration with lymphoid cells and plasma cells. Serum electrophoresis showed a large number of high molecular-weight monoclonal IgM proteins (greater than 3 gm/dl). What is the diagnosis?

*Your Own Answer*_____

Q419

What single agent treatment is best for a patient with psoriasis and psoriatic arthritis?

*Your Own Answer*_____

Q420

Dysplastic nevi is associated with an increased incidence of what type of transformation?

*Your Own Answer*_____

Correct Answers

Waldendstrom's macroglobulinemia (primary macro- **A418**
globulinemia) is associated with uncontrolled proliferation of lymphocytes and plasma cells, of which a large
number of high molecular-weight monoclonal IgM proteins
is produced. Retinal hemorrhages, exudates, and venous
congestion with vascular segmentation may occur. All patients have anemia. Males are more commonly affected.
Multiple myeloma, chronic lymphocytic leukemia and hy-
perviscosity syndrome can all present similarly, but elevation of the serum IgM protein is not present.

A419
Psoriasis has different treatment options. Light treatment, including UVB and PUVA, are well known treatments for psoriasis. Methotrexate and Imuran are
used as immune modulators in psoriasis. However,
only methotrexate is used in arthritis. Therefore, it is
the right choice for both psoriasis and psoriatic arthritis.

A420

Dysplastic nevi and congenital nevi are associated with an increased incidence of transformation to malignant melanoma.

Questions

Q421

What releases myocardial depressant factor?

*Your Own Answer*_____

Q422

Since sensory nerve fibers supplying the pancreas enter the spinal cord at T5-T9 levels, where is the pain associated with pancreatic cancer often referred?

*Your Own Answer*_____

Q423

Large, bruise-like subcutaneous hemorrhage is referred to by what term?

*Your Own Answer*_____

Correct Answers

A421

The pancreas releases the myocardial depressant factor, which often results in a depression
of contractility in the absence of necrosis following reperfusion injury in a subendocardial infarction.

A422

The pain from pancreatic cancer is often referred
to the inferior interscapular region, due to the
location of the T5 to T9 dermatomes on the back.

A423

Ecchymosis is a large, bruise-like hemorrhage in
the skin or subcutaneous tissue, which is visible
on physical exam.

Questions

Q424

Which antigen-presenting cells are associated with Peyer's patches?

*Your Own Answer*_____

Q425

Cardiac arrhythmia is a serious side effect of what drug used to treat bipolar disorder?

*Your Own Answer*_____

Q426

A 34-year-old male is in the intensive care unit after a motor vehicle accident. He is in a coma and is receiving enteral feedings through a jejunostomy tube. After several days, diarrhea started to occur. What are the causes of diarrhea secondary to enteral feedings?

*Your Own Answer*_____

Correct Answers

A424

Epithelial, cuboidal M-cells in the ileum function as antigen-presenting cells for T-lymphocytes in large collections of lymphatic nodules (Peyer's patches).

A425

Cardiac arrhythmia is a recognized sign of toxicity with lithium. Other side effects include tremor and vomiting.

A426

Hypertonic feedings cause high osmolality, and thus osmolar diarrhea. Bacterial contamination of feedings can cause infectious diarrhea. Refrigeration of formula and strict handwashing are necessary. Decrease in the acidity of the bowel by H2 blockers can alter the bowel flora and cause diarrhea. Antibiotics can also alter the bowel flora and cause *C difficile* diarrhea.

Questions

Q427

A 59-year-old woman with a history of chronic atrial fibrillation presents with hematuria, epistaxis, and easy bruiseability. She has been taking warfarin for several years to prevent embolization from atrial fibrillation. Her INR was greater than 5.0. What medication counteracts the effects of warfarin to prevent further bleeding episodes?

*Your Own Answer*_____

Q428

What is the etiology for cat-scratch disease?

*Your Own Answer*_____

Q429

Respiratory distress syndrome (hyaline membrane disease) in newborns results from which type of deficiency?

*Your Own Answer*_____

Correct Answers

A427

Hemorrhage secondary to warfarin can be reversed by administration of vitamin K by IV or by the subcutaneous route. This will reduce the prothrombin time and international normalization ratio (INR), but will take several days, since warfarin has a long half-life.

A428

Cat-scratch disease is caused by *Bartonella* (formerly Rochalimaea) *henselae* according to recent studies. It presents with regional lymphadenopathy, fever, and generalized malaise. Most frequently the vector animal is a cat. The primary lesion is usually a papule or a pustule on the arm or the hand.

A429

In respiratory distress syndrome of newborns, the Type II alveolar cells are immature and a deficiency in surfactant production results.

Questions

Q430

What are three features of lipoid proteinosis?

*Your Own Answer*_____

Q431

The superior mesenteric artery passes just anterior to which portion of the pancreas?

*Your Own Answer*_____

Q432

Amoeba, trypanosoma, leishmania, and schistosomas are all what type of organism?

*Your Own Answer*_____

Correct Answers

A430

Lipoid proteinosis presents with hyaline deposits under the skin and the mucosa. It can affect the buccal mucosa as well as throat and vocal cords. The lesions are waxy and translucent and they may present with a bead-like pattern perioculary and periorally. Hoarseness of the voice and firmness in the tongue, as well as calcification in the hippocampus in the brain and hair loss, are prominent features.

A431

The superior mesenteric artery passes posterior to the neck/body of the pancreas, but then anterior to the uncinate process (lingula).

A432

The protozoan is a single-cell organism. Amoeba, trypanosoma, leishmania, and schistosomas are all protozoa.

Questions

Q433

What are common features of malignant tumors?

*Your Own Answer*_____

Q434

Why must blood levels of aminoglycosides be closely monitored?

*Your Own Answer*_____

Q435

In cancer of the breast, the metastasis could possibly spread to which lymphatic sites?

*Your Own Answer*_____

Correct Answers

A433

Malignant tumors are more likely to have a higher number of mitotic figures compared to benign tumors. Malignant tumors are also often poorly differentiated, locally invasive, able to metastasize, and have an irregular invasive structure.

A434

Nephrotoxicity and ototoxicity are both known side effects of treatment with aminoglycosides such as gentamicin.

A435

The axillary nodes, the parasternal lymph nodes, the abdominal nodes, and the opposite breast could potentially receive metastases from a cancerous breast, because its lymphatics drain to all these sites.

Questions

Q436

During surgery to drain and close a rectal fistula located in the ischiorectal fossa, care must be taken not to damage which structures?

*Your Own Answer*_____

Q437

What has a higher Linear Energy Transfer (LET) value than X-rays, gamma rays, protons, and beta particles.

*Your Own Answer*_____

Q438

A 45-year-old white male smoker visits his primary care physician for a routine exam. His serum cholesterol level was 350 mg/dl. His blood pressure was 160/96 mmHg. This patient has a family history of heart disease and he also leads a sedentary lifestyle. The National Cholesterol Education Program recommends dietary modification if two consecutive LDL cholesterol levels are above what level?

*Your Own Answer*_____

Correct Answers

A436

The inferior rectal nerves, branches of the pudendal nerve, traverse the ischiorectal (ischioanal) fossa, and would be vulnerable in this invasive procedure.

A437

Linear energy transfer is the value that indicates the radiation's likelihood of having an effect within a certain area. It is determined by charge and by mass. Alpha particles have a higher LET because they have a larger mass and a higher charge than the others.

A438

Dietary measures are also recommended if two LDL determinations are 130 to 159 mg/dl when the patient has two or more risk factors for coronary heart disease. Low HDL levels (less than 35 mg/dl) are a risk factor for heart disease.

Questions

Q439

What would be the result of a patent ductus arteriosus?

*Your Own Answer*_____

Q440

A tumor of chromaffin cells in the adrenal medulla would result in the release of excessive levels of what substance into the bloodstream?

*Your Own Answer*_____

Q441

What structure passes anterior to the aorta and posterior to the superior mesenteric artery?

*Your Own Answer*_____

Correct Answers

A439

With a patent ductus arteriosus, arterial blood from the aorta would flow into the pulmonary artery via the ductus arteriosus. This high-pressure perfusion of the lungs with blood from the aorta would lead to pulmonary hypertension, increased pressure in the pulmonary circulation, which is fatal if not surgically corrected.

A440

A tumor of chromaffin cells in the adrenal medulla (pheochromocytoma) typically results in excessive secretion of epinephrine into the blood.

A441

The uncinate process of the pancreas is crossed posteriorly by the aorta and anteriorly by the superior mesenteric artery.

Questions

Q442

A mutation of which gene is associated with an X-linked recessive disorder characterized by spastic uncontrolled movements and self-mutilation?

*Your Own Answer*_____

Q443

Where in the body is vitamin B12 is absorbed?

*Your Own Answer*_____

Q444

A 43-year-old female was found on the street by a neighbor after having fallen from a syncopal attack. In the hospital, her supine blood pressure was 120/70 mm Hg, and upright the blood pressure was 90/70 mm Hg. Many tests, including a Holter monitor and electrocardiogram, were negative. A seizure work-up was negative. What is a useful diagnostic test to determine the cause of her attack?

*Your Own Answer*_____

Correct Answers

A442

Lesch-Nyhan syndrome is an X-linked recessive disorder that is caused by a defect in the HPRT gene, which is needed for the purine salvage pathway. The disorder results in excess uric acid production, spastic uncontrolled movements, self-mutilation, mental retardation, and hematologic dysfunction.

A443

Vitamin B_{12} is essential for cell growth and for maintaining normal myelin. It is normally absorbed in the ileum in three steps. First, gastric acid in the stomach frees B_{12} from proteins. Next, it binds to Intrinsic Factor in the stomach. Third, it binds to ileal mucosal cell receptors and is then absorbed.

A444

For 20 years, head-up tilt table testing has been used to assess orthostatic hypotension. This maneuver may evoke the symptoms for which the patient seeks help, including intermittent confusion due to hypoxemia cerebrally, and unexplained syncope. Tilt table testing is particularly useful in elderly patients who have been fully worked up but have unexplained transient ischemic attacks or unexplained seizures.

Questions

Q445

Venous blood from the pituitary gland empties directly into which dural venous sinus?

*Your Own Answer*_____

Q446

A 36-year-old pregnant woman presents with abdominal pain and mild jaundice. Physical exam is significant for hepatomegaly. Hepatic venography demonstrates thrombosis of the hepatic veins. What is the most likely diagnosis?

*Your Own Answer*_____

Q447

In scurvy, which results from a vitamin C deficiency, what is defectively produced by fibroblasts, resulting in a generalized breakdown of connective tissue in the body?

*Your Own Answer*_____

Correct Answers

A445

The veins draining the pituitary gland empty into the cavernous sinus.

A446

Budd-Chiari syndrome is a complication of hypercoagulable states, such as pregnancy, resulting in thrombosis of the hepatic veins. If untreated, it can progress to liver failure.

A447

Vitamin C deficiency ultimately results in the formation of defective collagen fibers by fibroblasts.

Questions

Q448

During nerve regeneration, what is produced by macrophages, stimulating Schwann cells to produce nerve growth factor?

*Your Own Answer*_____

Q449

What is a typical formation for streptococcus ssp?

*Your Own Answer*_____

Q450

What drug was recently approved by FDA for onychomycosis?

*Your Own Answer*_____

Correct Answers

A448

Interleukin-1 is a cytokine produced by macrophages that stimulates Schwann cells to produce nerve growth factor.

A449

Gram-positive cocci in chains.

A450

The only FDA-approved oral antifungal for onychomycosis was Griseofulvin, until recently, when itraconazole was approved.

Questions

Q451

What is the most important risk factor for developing atherosclerosis for men over the age of 45?

*Your Own Answer*_____

Q452

Esophageal varices, caput medusae, and hemorrhoids can all result from pathology related to which structure?

*Your Own Answer*_____

Q453

When is the viscosity of cervical mucus at a peak?

*Your Own Answer*_____

Correct Answers

A451

Hypertension is the most important risk factor for developing atherosclerosis for people over the age of 45. Hyperlipidemia is the most important risk factor for those under 45 years of age. Cigarette smoking, diabetes mellitus, obesity, sedentary life style, type A personality, and oral contraceptive use are other risk factors.

A452

Liver pathology typically leads to portal hypertension, causing the signs listed.

A453

The viscosity of the mucous secretion of the cervical glands (Nabothian glands) is highest just prior to ovulation.

Questions

Q454

Patients with phenylketonuria have a deficiency of what enzyme?

*Your Own Answer*_____

Q455

The proximal portion of the jejunum is supported by a thickened slip of peritoneum. What is this known as?

*Your Own Answer*_____

Q456

Dysphagia is most commonly associated with which malignancy?

*Your Own Answer*_____

Correct Answers

A454

Phenylketonurics cannot convert phenylalanine to tyrosine because of deficiency of phenylalanine hydroxylase.

A455

The ligament of Treitz, also known as the suspensory ligament (muscle) of the duodenum, extends from the right crus of the diaphragm to the duodenal-jejunal junction.

A456

Dysphagia means difficulty swallowing; it is one of the cardinal signs of esophageal cancer.

Questions

Q457

A patient who recently had a coronary artery bypass graft (CABG) complains of abnormal sensations (tingling, burning, numbness, etc.) along the medial aspect of the leg from the medial malleolus to the medial condyle of the tibia. When the distal portion of the great saphenous vein was harvested for the CABG, what nerve was inadvertently damaged?

*Your Own Answer*_____

_____

Q458

A swallowed (aspirated) object that accidentally enters the trachea would likely eventually lodge where?

*Your Own Answer*_____

_____

Q459

Carcinoid tumors in the liver metabolize which amino acid to produce excess urinary 5-hydroxyindoleacetic acid (5-HIAA)?

*Your Own Answer*_____

_____

Correct Answers

A457

The saphenous nerve runs in close proximity to the greater saphenous vein in the leg, and is thus vulnerable when the vein is harvested.

A458

Most often, an aspirated object entering the trachea will lodge in the right main bronchus, because it is wider, shorter, and more vertical than the left main bronchus.

A459

Tryptophan is hydroxylated and then decarboxylated to produce serotonin, which is then deaminated and oxidized to produce 5-hydroxyindoleacetic acid (5-HIAA), which is detected in the urine. Excess 5-HIAA produces the carcinoid syndrome, characterized by flushing, diarrhea, and bronchoconstriction.

Questions

Q460

A concerned mother brings her child into the emergency room after she notices her child presenting one-to-two second seizures, which are characterized by a blank stare. During the seizures, the child's head droops and the arms jerk in a rhythmic manner. For alleviation of the symptoms, which pharamacologic agent is most likely to be prescribed?

*Your Own Answer*_____

Q461

In a population at equilibrium, three genotypes are present in the following proportions: A/A 0.81, *a*/*a* 0.01, where A and *a* are two alleles of a certain gene. What is the frequency of allele A/*a* in the population?

*Your Own Answer*_____

Q462

A gunshot wound that damages the mid-portion greater curvature of the stomach would likely produce extensive bleeding from what artery?

*Your Own Answer*_____

Correct Answers

A460

Ethosuximide is the only drug solely indicated for petit mal, or absence seizures of epilepsy, and would most likely be prescribed.

A461

From the Hardy-Weinberg Law, the sum of the genotype frequencies must equal 1, so the heterozygote frequency is $1 - A^2 - a^2 = 0.18$. Equivalently, the heterozygote frequency is given by $2Aa$, which equals $2(0.9)(0.1) = 0.18$.

A462

The left gastroepiploic artery, which descends along the greater curvature of the stomach and anastomoses with the right gastroepiploic artery, would likely bleed extensively.

Questions

Q463

In a male patient with a severe gonorrheal venereal infection, it is found that urine is collecting in the deep perineal space. This suggests a perforation in the wall of which structure?

Your Own Answer_____

Q464

A traumatic wound in the neck has resulted in a loss of sensory innervation to the mucosa of the false (vestibular) vocal fold in the larynx. What nerve was damaged by the injury?

Your Own Answer_____

Q465

What anti-parasitic drug will exacerbate psoriasis?

Your Own Answer_____

Correct Answers

A463

The deep perineal space that lies between the superior and inferior fascia of the urogenital diaphragm. Since the membranous urethra passes through the urogenital diaphragm, a perforation of the membranous urethra could result in the collection of urine in the deep perineal space.

A464

The injury damaged the internal laryngeal nerve, which supplies the laryngeal mucosa above the vocal folds.

A465

Chloroquine, an anti-malarial medicine, which is used in lupus, exacerbates psoriasis.

Questions

Q466

In the abdominal cavity, the greater sac communicates with the lesser sac via which structure?

*Your Own Answer*_____

Q467

Neurogenic vasoconstriction in arterioles is usually the direct result of what?

*Your Own Answer*_____

Q468

A 35-year-old woman is brought to the emergency room because of a bleeding gastric ulcer. She is anemic and losing blood continuously. Her physician recommends four units of packed red blood cells to be transfused immediately. What complications are associated with transfusing the four units of blood?

*Your Own Answer*_____

Correct Answers

A466

The opening into the lesser sac from the greater sac is the epiploic foramen of Winslow.

A467

Sympathetic innervation usually results in neurogenic vasoconstriction in arterioles.

A468

Infections, such as HIV, hepatitis B, and non-A, non-B hepatitis, can potentially occur after a blood transfusion, but this is rare because of donor screening programs. Potentially fatal transfusion reactions can occur and be immediate or delayed. CMV exposure can occur after transfusions and with transplantation of organs. Pulmonary leukoagglutinin reaction after a blood transfusion is very rare, but it can occur.

Questions

Q469

What causes ecthyma?

Your Own Answer _____

Q470

What is caused by zinc deficiency?

Your Own Answer _____

Q471

A 68-year-old male was hospitalized because of acute abdomen pain secondary to pancreatitis. There were no stones or sludge visualized by endoscopic retrograde pancreatography. The patient denies alcohol use. On exam, there were prominent nodules on the elbows and "whitish" vessels seen in the optic fundus. No spider angiomas, splenomegaly, testicular atrophy, or clinical ascites were present. What is the most likely diagnosis?

Your Own Answer _____

Correct Answers

A469

Echtyma is a deep form of impetigo with ulceratino and scarring, which is caused by *Staphylococcus aureus* or streptococci.

A470

Acrodermatitis enterohepatica is an autosomal recessive disease. It is caused by zinc insufficiency in infancy. It is characterized by acrodermatitis, alopecia and diarrhea.

A471

Hyperlipoproteinemia I, also known as extreme hypertriglyceridemia (with levels exceeding 1,000 mg/dl), can cause pancreatitis, lipemia retinalis, and tuberous xanthomas.

Questions

Q472

In a normal 22-year-old woman, which type of follicular cell would be the most numerous in her ovaries at any given time?

*Your Own Answer*_____

Q473

A patient with frequent mood shifts, unstable relationships, and who is subject to episodes of extreme rage, but who maintains a steady job and has no other overt psychopathology, might be diagnosed with which disorder?

*Your Own Answer*_____

Q474

What is a nitrogenous base found in RNA molecules but not DNA molecules?

*Your Own Answer*_____

Correct Answers

A472

Each ovary contains about 200,000 primordial follicles in a young adult woman, thus greatly outnumbering all of the other stages of follicular development.

A473

Borderline personality-disorder patients can be very difficult to interact with because of violently shifting moods. However, they are often able to lead fairly normal lives without manifesting acute psychiatric disorders.

A474

Uracil is a base found in RNA molecules, and is the DNA equivalent of thymine. Adenine and guanine are DNA purine bases (double-ring formation), while cytosine and thymine are DNA pyrimidine bases (single-ring formation).

Questions

Q475

What is the shape of the virus that causes rabies?

*Your Own Answer*_____

Q476

The clumped, shrunken appearance of chromatin associated with basophilia seen in ischemic cell injury is referred to by what term?

*Your Own Answer*_____

Q477

What is the etiology for Rocky Mountain spotted fever?

*Your Own Answer*_____

Correct Answers

A475

Rabies is caused by rhabdovirus, which is the only bullet-shaped virus. It is also an enveloped virus containing RNA.

A476

Pyknosis refers to the clumped chromatin and basophilia seen with ischemic cell injury.

A477

Rocky Mountain spotted fever is caused by *Rickettsia rickettsii* and it is transmitted by a tick bite.

Questions

Q478

Where should a stethoscope be placed in order to hear the sounds of the aortic valve ?

*Your Own Answer*_____

Q479

What is the best indicator of the poorest prognosis in an HIV-infected patient?

*Your Own Answer*_____

Q480

A tumor of the choroid plexus could lead to an overproduction of which substance?

*Your Own Answer*_____

Correct Answers

A478

Using a stethoscope, the aortic valve is auscultated at the sternal end of the right 2nd intercostal space.

A479

Polymerase chain reaction measurement of plasma HIV RNA (viral load) is actually a far more powerful prognostic indicator of mortality for AIDS than the CD4 count. CD4 lymphocyte counts are useful in determining the rate of progression of HIV infection, but the viral load measurement is better.

A480

Cerebrospinal fluid is produced by the choroid plexus. A tumor could lead to its overproduction.

Questions

Q481

The Philadelphia chromosome, Ph1, is associated with which type of malignancy?

*Your Own Answer*_____

Q482

Your patient has a tumor of gastrin-producing enteroendocrine cells (G-cells). What might this particular tumor result in, assuming the tumor is producing excessive amounts of gastrin?

*Your Own Answer*_____

Q483

A chest X ray shows a mass in the lingular segment of a lung. What lobe contains the mass?

*Your Own Answer*_____

Correct Answers

A481

The Philadelphia chromosome is associated with both acute and chronic leukemias, particularly chronic myeloid leukemia.

A482

Gastrin promotes HCl and gastric intrinsic factor production by parietal cells in the gastric glands; thus, in this case, excess HCl production would occur.

A483

The left upper lobe contains the lingular segment and, thus, the mass.

Questions

Q484

What is the most common cutaneous eruption during pregnancy?

*Your Own Answer*_____

Q485

What is used to treat condyloma acuminata?

*Your Own Answer*_____

Q486

What is the hypothesis that states that one X chromosome is inactivated in females ?

*Your Own Answer*_____

Correct Answers

A484

Pruritic urticarial papules and plaques of pregnancy, also known as PUPPP, is the most common cutaneous problem during pregnancy, and is usually seen in the third trimester of pregnancy. They usually start on the abdomen along the striae distensa lines around the umbilicus. They are very pruritic and they usually resolve with birth.

A485

Condyloma acuminata are genital warts of viral etiology. They can be treated by cryosurgery and electrodesiccation, which are destruction methods. Podophyllin is another way of treating condyloma acuminata, as well as Condylox, which is the prescription form of podophyllin.

A486

The Lyon hypothesis states that in females, one X chromosome is inactivated, thus equalizing the expression of X-linked genes in the female. This is why X-linked disorders are more severe in males. In females, the defective gene on one X chromosome is not 100% expressed, as it is in males.

Questions

Q487

Infectious mononucleosis is most commonly caused by which virus?

*Your Own Answer*_____

Q488

A 61-year-old man is admitted to a hospital with pneumococcal pneumonia. Several hours after admission he demonstrates circulatory collapse and has a cardiac arrest. A blood culture taken shortly after admission demonstrates pneumococci in the blood. What is the most likely diagnosis?

*Your Own Answer*_____

Q489

A patient has sustained a gunshot wound in the chest. In the hilus of the right lung, the bullet is lodged in a structure lying just superior to the right pulmonary artery. What structure is the bullet lodged in?

*Your Own Answer*_____

Correct Answers

A487

Epstein-Barr virus is the most common cause of infectious mononucleosis and may also play a role in chronic-fatigue syndrome. Mononucleosis may also be caused by cytomegalovirus.

A488

The most likely diagnosis given this history is septic shock. *Streptococcus pneumoniae* can cause bacteremia and septic shock.

A489

In the hilus of the right lung, the right primary bronchus lies just superior to the right pulmonary artery.

Questions

Q490

The most common oral cancer is characterized by what histology?

Your Own Answer_____

Q491

A squamous cell carcinoma in the scrotum would likely result in metastasis to which nodes?

Your Own Answer_____

Q492

A surgical specimen of a normal palatine tonsil would possess what distinctive characteristic?

Your Own Answer_____

Correct Answers

A490

Over 90% of oral cancers have a squamous cell histology, and alcohol and tobacco increase the risk of developing such a cancer.

A491

Metastasis would spread to the superficial inguinal nodes into which the lymphatics of the scrotum directly drain.

A492

A diagnostic feature of the palatine tonsils is the presence of deep invaginations of its surface lined by stratified squamous epithelium.

Questions

Q493

Damage to which structure would result in loss of control of the external sphincter of the urethra?

*Your Own Answer*_____

Q494

A stab wound in the anterior abdominal wall 2 cm lateral to the midline and below the arcuate line would damage which tissue layer just deep of the rectus abdominis?

*Your Own Answer*_____

Q495

Rogaine takes advantage of one of the side effects (hypertrichosis) of minoxidil, an anti-hypertensive agent. What other major side effect does minoxidil have?

*Your Own Answer*_____

Correct Answers

A493

The pudendal nerve supplies voluntary motor innervation to the external urethral sphincter. Damage to this nerve would result in loss of control of the external urethral sphincter.

A494

The transversalis fascia would be damaged, due to the absence of the rectus sheath below the arcuate line deep to the rectus abdominis, leaving only the transversalis fascia exposed, which covers the parietal peritoneum.

A495

The other major side effect of minoxidil is orthostatic hypertension.

Questions

Q496

A 64-year-old woman slipped and fell on the ice. She was rushed to the local hospital and X rays were taken. This patient has no past medical history except osteoporosis. Which fracture is her physician most likely to find?

*Your Own Answer*_____

Q497

What drug is indicated for delusions of parasitosis?

*Your Own Answer*_____

Q498

Decreased activity of a1-antitrypsin is most associated with which disorder?

*Your Own Answer*_____

Correct Answers

A496

Women 51 to 75 years of age are at risk for Type 1 osteoporosis, which is characterized by the loss of a greater amount of trabecular bone than cortical bone. The loss of trabecular bone mass puts the patient at risk for Colles' fracture (fracture of the distal radius) and verterbral crush fractures.

A497

Pimozide is proven to be effective for delusions of parasitosis.

A498

a1-antitrypsin is a major plasma protease inhibitor that acts on neutrophil elastase (NE) in the lung. NE is released from activated neutrophils during acute inflammation and destroys the agents of inflammation along with normal structures, such as alveolar walls. a1-antitrypsin protects the wall from NE-induced damage, and a defect in a1-antitrypsin may result in emphysema.

Questions

Q499

While the adrenal cortex is partly under the influence of the pituitary gland, what directly controls the adrenal medulla?

*Your Own Answer*_____

Q500

What results in edema that is high in protein content (exudate) rather than low in protein content (transudate)?

*Your Own Answer*_____

Q501

To increase muscle mass and overall strength, a football player initiates an intense program of weight lifting. What effect will this have on his muscles after a few weeks of training?

*Your Own Answer*_____

Correct Answers

A499

The chromaffin cells of the adrenal medulla receive preganglionic sympathetic (splanchnic) nerve fibers. Thus, these nerves play a direct regulatory role in adrenal medullary function.

A500

Increased capillary permeability may be caused by inflammation, and results in edema characterized by a high protein content (exudate). Lymphatic obstruction, increased salt and water retention, increased venous hydrostatic pressure, and decreased plasma-oncotic pressure all result in edema characterized by low protein content (transudate).

A501

Skeletal muscle cells will undergo hypertrophy (enlarge) as a result of intense exercise.

Questions

Q502

What is the effect of botulism toxin on the release of acetylcholine at the neuromuscular synapse?

*Your Own Answer*_____

Q503

A 60-year-old man with a history of coronary artery disease presents with abdominal pain. On physical examination he is found to be hypotensive and have a pulsatile mass in the midline of his abdomen. What is the most likely diagnosis?

*Your Own Answer*_____

Q504

The growth of the endometrium during the proliferative phase of the uterine cycle correlates with what activity?

*Your Own Answer*_____

Correct Answers

A502

Botulism toxin, produced by *Clostridium botulinum*, inhibits the release of acetylcholine, producing a flaccid paralysis.

A503

Rupturing abdominal aortic aneurysm presents as a pulsatile mass in the midline of the abdomen. This condition is a surgical emergency with a high mortality rate.

A504

The proliferative phase of the uterine cycle correlates with the secretion of estradiol by growing ovarian follicles.

Questions

In cardiac muscle, what are intercalated disks?

*Your Own Answer*_____

What food-borne bacterial disease is commonly found in fishermen, butchers, or people who deal with meat products?

*Your Own Answer*_____

An Rh-negative woman married to a heterozygous Rh-positive man has three children. What is the probability that at least one of their children is Rh-positive?

*Your Own Answer*_____

Correct Answers

A505

Intercalated disks are the junctional complexes between adjacent muscle cells.

A506

Erysipeloid is caused *by Erysipelothrix rhusiopathiae* and is a Gram-positive rod mostly seen in fishermen, butchers, or people handling raw fish, poultry, and meat products. It is an erythematous violaceous nodule, usually on the fingers. It is accompanied by regional lymphadenopathy.

A507

P(at least one child is Rh-positive) = 1 - P(all three children are Rh-negative). P(all three children are Rh-negative) = $1/2 \times 1/2 \times 1/2 = 1/8$, and $1 - 1/8 = 7/8$.

Questions

Q508

A 46-year-old man presents with fever, chills, and hepatomegaly. History is significant for a recent trip on which he spent several weeks in the Far East. Hepatic imaging shows dilatation of the bile ducts. Stool samples contain what appear to be eggs. The most likely diagnosis is infection with which parasite?

*Your Own Answer*_____

Q509

What gives rise to the anterior interventricular (left anterior descending) coronary artery?

*Your Own Answer*_____

Q510

Which nerves supply parasympathetic innervation to the hindgut?

*Your Own Answer*_____

Correct Answers

A508

Clonorchis sinensis, also known as liver fluke, causes parasitic infection in man. Infection is often associated with ingestion of raw fish; larvae from the fish localize to the liver.

A509

The left coronary artery gives rise to the anterior interventricular artery.

A510

The hindgut (distal to transverse colon) is supplied by pelvic splanchnic nerves (parasympathetic).

Questions

Q511

What is the major side effect of antihistamines?

*Your Own Answer*_____

_____

Q512

An otherwise healthy 25-year-old woman presents with renal stones. Her history is not significant for any previous stone disease or risk factors for stone formation. On further questioning, she admits to taking high doses of vitamins and other supplements. What is the most likely diagnosis?

*Your Own Answer*_____

_____

Q513

A severe inversion injury of the foot could result in the avulsion of a tendon inserting into the tuberosity on the base of the 5th metatarsal bone. What muscle's tendon inserts here?

*Your Own Answer*_____

_____

Correct Answers

A511

Antihistamines cause drowsiness as a side effect. Newer antihistamines such as loratadine and terfenadine effectively block histamines' effects with less sedation.

A512

Hypervitaminosis D leads to hypercalcuria and stone formation.

A513

The peroneus brevis inserts at the base of the 5th metatarsal, and is thus a common site of an avulsion injury when the foot is violently inverted.

Questions

Q514

Where are Osler's nodes seen?

Your Own Answer_____

Q515

When ligating the uterine artery during a hysterectomy, care must be taken not to damage which structure, passing directly posterior and inferior to the uterine artery?

Your Own Answer_____

Q516

A 54-year-old patient with congestive heart failure presents with pedal edema (edema of the ankles). How would this edema fluid be considered?

Your Own Answer_____

Correct Answers

A514

The cutaneous manifestations of subacute bacterial endocarditis include petechiae, subungual splinter hemorrhages, and Osler's nodes, which are small, erythematous, painful nodular lesions usually on the fingerpads and toes and over the arms. They are transient and last about 12 to 24 hours.

A515

A key relationship in the female pelvic cavity that must be recognized surgically is the crossing of the uterine artery by the ureter.

A516

A transudate is fluid that escapes from the vascular space due to changes in pressure. In this patient, intravascular volume is increased, so fluid seeps into surrounding tissues.

Questions

Q517

What is the leading cause of death in the United States?

*Your Own Answer*_____

Q518

A 58-year-old white female presents with severe substernal chest pain radiating to her left shoulder and associated with shortness of breath, diaphoresis, and nausea. Her electrocardiogram revealed ST-T wave elevations in the inferior leads, suggesting an MI. What type of therapy may decrease her risk of death?

*Your Own Answer*_____

Q519

A three-year-old male presents with splenomegaly and severe neurologic abnormalities. Bone marrow aspirate demonstrates reticulum cell hyperplasia. Cell culture demonstrates lack of glucocerebrosidase activity. What is the most likely diagnosis?

*Your Own Answer*_____

Correct Answers

A517

Atherosclerosis and its complications (e.g., stroke, myocardial infarction) is the leading cause of death in the United States.

A518

In-hospital mortality rates following acute myocardial infarction has declined more than 50% over the past 25 years, and one-year mortality rates continue to decrease. This is due largely to thrombolytic therapy given within 4 to 6 hours of the onset of chest pain.

A519

Gaucher's disease is lipid storage disease characterized by a lack of glucocerebrosidase activity, which can lead to severe neurologic abnormalities.

Questions

Q520

Your patient has abnormally high blood pressure resulting from a tumor of the adrenal cortex. Where is the tumor localized?

*Your Own Answer*_____

Q521

What neoplasm is associated with necrolytic migratory erythema?

*Your Own Answer*_____

Q522

In a biopsy slide of an underactive thyroid gland, what characteristic would be evident?

*Your Own Answer*_____

Correct Answers

A520

The tumor is localized in the zona glomerulosa, where it would cause a large increase in blood aldosterone levels, leading to increased sodium reabsorption by the distal convoluted tubules in the kidneys, and thus increased blood pressure.

A521

Necrolytic migratory erythema presents with scaly erythema and sometimes with vesicles and bullae involving the face as well as the intertriginous areas and the rest of the extremities. Sometimes it looks like psoriasis. It can be associated with flossitis or alopecia. It is a sign of glucagon-producing tumor.

A522

In an underactive thyroid, the synthesis of thyroglobulin and colloid continues, resulting in an increase in the size (diameter) of the follicles due to an increase in the volume of stored colloid.

Questions

Q523

In histological sections, how do Purkinje fibers in the heart appear?

*Your Own Answer*_____

Q524

In Horner's syndrome, what causes the flushing and warmth of the skin of the face?

*Your Own Answer*_____

Q525

In pulmonary vascular congestion, hemosiderin pigment accumulates in what cell type within the lungs?

*Your Own Answer*_____

Correct Answers

A523

Purkinje fibers in the heart appear as swollen, lightly-staining cardiac muscle fibers. Their modified cardiac muscle cells conduct electrical impulses initiated by the sinoatrial node.

A524

The flushing results from vasodilation due to loss of sympathetic innervation of arterioles in the skin.

A525

Alveolar macrophages ingest extravasated red blood cells and subsequently exhibit hemosiderin pigment granules in the cytoplasm.

Questions

Q526

Bell's palsy results from impairment of which cranial nerve?

*Your Own Answer*_____

Q527

When doing an intragluteal injection, what muscle should be injected?

*Your Own Answer*_____

Q528

A patient with apical lung cancer presents with hoarseness due to paralysis of the vocal folds. The cancer has resulted in damage to what nerve, because of its intimate relationship to the apex of the right lung?

*Your Own Answer*_____

Correct Answers

A526

Bell's palsy, facial paralysis, results from impairment of cranial nerve VII, the facial nerve.

A527

Intragluteal injections should always be performed in the superior lateral quadrant of the gluteal region, in the gluteus medius, to avoid damage to the sciatic nerve.

A528

A lesion of the apex of the right lung would potentially involve the recurrent laryngeal nerve, which crosses the inferior surface of the right subclavian artery, producing hoarseness associated with paralysis of the intrinsic laryngeal muscles on the right side.

Questions

Q529

Malignant ovarian cancer would initially metastasize to which nodes?

*Your Own Answer*_____

Q530

Impetigo herpetiformis is usually seen in which trimester of pregnancy?

*Your Own Answer*_____

Q531

What structure would be most vulnerable to damage (by bone fragments) if the shaft of the fibula is broken by a lateral blow midway down the leg?

*Your Own Answer*_____

Correct Answers

A529

Since the lymphatics draining the ovary follow the ovary artery back to the aorta, ovarian cancer would initially metastasize to the para-aortic nodes.

A530

Impetigo herpetiformis is a kind of pustular psoriasis that can happen during pregnancy. It is usually seen in the third trimester of pregnancy.

A531

The peroneal artery and vein, both lying directly medial to the fibula, would be vulnerable when the shaft of the bone is fractured.

Questions

Q532

What disease is caused by a defect in the DNA helicase gene?

*Your Own Answer*_____

Q533

What is the chief function of the corpus luteum during the menstrual cycle?

*Your Own Answer*_____

Q534

A patient receives a blood transfusion and develops a severe hemolytic anemia, hematuria, and back pain. What type of immunologic reaction is this?

*Your Own Answer*_____

Correct Answers

A532

Werner's syndrome is characterized by a premature onset of aging and is caused by a defect in the DNA helicase gene needed for nucleotide excision repair.

A533

The corpus luteum prepares the uterus for implantation by producing large quantities of progesterone and estradiol, both of which enhance the secretion of uterine glands, and provide an optimal microenvironment for implantation of the zygote once it reaches the uterus.

A534

Blood transfusion reactions occur when circulating IgG or IgM antibodies recognize cell-surface antigens. This interaction then causes complement activation. This is known as a type II immune reaction.

Questions

Q535

What primary bullous disease presents with a flaccid bullae?

*Your Own Answer*_____

Q536

Comedones are associated with what disease?

*Your Own Answer*_____

Q537

Your patient has a bacterial infection that is spreading within the superficial fascia of the leg. What structure associated with peripheral nerves would prevent the spread of bacteria from connective tissue to the endoneurium?

*Your Own Answer*_____

Correct Answers

A535

All primary bullous diseases of the skin manifest with a tense blister, except pemphigus vulgaris, which has a flaccid blister.

A536

Comedomes are associated with acne vulgaris.

A537

Due to its layer of epithelial-like cells with tight junctions, basal laminae, and pinocytic vesicles, the perineurium prevents large-molecular weight substances from entering the endoneurium from outside the nerve fascicle.

Questions

Rifampin is used to treat what disease?

*Your Own Answer*_____

What is the inheritance pattern of Hailey-Hailey disease?

*Your Own Answer*_____

A 52-year-old female presented to her physician with symptoms of polyuria, polydipsia, weakness, and malaise. Her fasting blood glucose level was 379 mg/dl. What treatment option lowers blood sugar by interfering with intestinal absorption of complex carbohydrates?

*Your Own Answer*_____

Correct Answers

A538

Rifampin has been used for tuberculosis for a long time and it is mycobacteriocidal.

A539

Hailey-Hailey is an autosomal dominant disease.

A540

Acarbose is an alpha-glucosidase inhibitor, which interferes with intestinal absorption of complex carbohydrates, and thus lowers the glucose load absorbed in the body. Alternatively, metformin is a biguanide, which works by decreasing hepatic glucose production by 30% and increasing glucose utilization in skeletal muscle.

Questions

Q541

Your patient has an autoimmune disease whereby there is a gradual destruction of C-cells (parafollicular cells) in the thyroid gland. What would be the result?

*Your Own Answer*_____

Q542

What is the name of the yellowish bands of platelets seen in the thrombus of a pulmonary embolus?

*Your Own Answer*_____

Q543

In an automobile accident, a woman received fractures of both pubic rami. What structure, just posterior to the pubis, is vulnerable in this type of injury?

*Your Own Answer*_____

Correct Answers

A541

Since the parafollicular (C-cells) of the thyroid produce calcitonin, a decrease in the number of C-cells would ultimately result in increased blood calcium levels.

A542

The lines of platelets are called Zahn platelets; they were named after Zahn.

A543

The urinary bladder lies directly posterior to the rami of the pubis, and thus would be vulnerable.

Questions

Q544

What is the main histological difference between the pulmonary artery and the pulmonary vein?

*Your Own Answer*_____

Q545

You have a patient that is unable to dorsiflex and invert his right foot. Where is the lesion?

*Your Own Answer*_____

Q546

In the epidermis, where does the secretion of cells create a waterproof barrier?

*Your Own Answer*_____

Correct Answers

A544

The pulmonary artery, like the aorta, is classified as a large, elastic artery because of the abundance of elastic lamellae (elastin polymers) in the tunica media. The pulmonary vein would differ by not having these lamellae in the tunica media.

A545

The lesion is on the deep peroneal nerve. An inability to dorsiflex and invert the foot indicates possible denervation of the tibialis anterior muscle, which is innervated by the deep peroneal nerve.

A546

The cells of the stratum granulosum contain lipid-rich lamellar bodies that, when exocytosed, form a water-proof protective barrier, preventing dehydration of the skin from loss of water, as well as over-hydration from water penetrating the surface of the skin.

Questions

Q547

What common disorder may be associated with granuloma annulare?

*Your Own Answer*_____

Q548

Because of its close relationship to the thyroid gland, which nerve is the most vulnerable to damage during thyroidectomy?

*Your Own Answer*_____

Q549

What test is diagnostic for histoplasmosis in the absence of skin lesions?

*Your Own Answer*_____

Correct Answers

A547

Granuloma annulare is a granulomatous skin condition, which may be associated with diabetes.

A548

The recurrent laryngeal nerve runs just posterior to the thyroid gland in the tracheoesophageal groove, and must be identified during thyroidectomy.

A549

If there are no skin lesions, the most useful diagnostic technique will be a bone marrow biopsy. Cutaneous lesions occur less than 10% of the time in disseminated histoplasmosis. However, oral lesions are more common. The treatment is Amphotericin B and ketoconazole.

Questions

Q550

Alkaptonuria is caused by what type of deficiency?

*Your Own Answer*_____

Q551

A 65-year-old female presented with a history of recent lower gastrointestinal bleeding. There is no associated abdominal pain, anorexia, or weight loss. On examination, she was tachycardic with a blood pressure of 90/70 mm Hg and she appeared pale. Rectal examination revealed bright red blood. Her hematocrit was 22%. There was no significant past medical history. She was given two units of blood to stabilize her. What is the most common cause for this patient's bleeding?

*Your Own Answer*_____

Q552

Cancer of the bladder would result in metastasis to which nodes?

*Your Own Answer*_____

Correct Answers

A550

Homogentisic oxidase deficiency causes alkaptonuria. This deficiency leads to accumulation of homogentisic acid; patients' urine turns black on standing.

A551

Diverticulosis is the most common cause of lower GI bleeding in this age group. Diverticular hemorrhage is characteristically painless and associated with large-volume hematochezia. Inflammation of the diverticuli causes diverticulitis.

A552

Metastasis would spread to the internal and external iliac nodes, into which the lymphatics of the bladder drain.

Questions

Q553

What DNA sequence codes for the tRNA antic-odon that binds to the UAG terminator codon?

*Your Own Answer*_____

Q554

Which cells are diagnostic of Hodgkin's lym-phoma?

*Your Own Answer*_____

Q555

The inguinal ligament is formed primarily by a thickening of the inferiolateral portion of which structure?

*Your Own Answer*_____

Correct Answers

A553

The process of protein synthesis involves transcription from DNA and then translation by tRNA. The anticodon for UAG is CUA (based on RNA base pairing). The DNA sequence that coded for CUA must thus be TAG (based on DNA pairing).

A554

Reed-Sternberg cells are reticuloendothelial cells with large, multinucleate cells with prominent nucleoli and are diagnostic of Hodgkin's lymphoma.

A555

The external oblique aponeurosis folds under at its inferior border to form the inguinal ligament.

Questions

Q556

The surface epithelium that covers Peyer's patches in the ileum is modified to form a simple cuboidal epithelium, consisting of M-cells. What is the function of M-cells?

*Your Own Answer*_____

Q557

What is a stable cell?

*Your Own Answer*_____

Q558

A three-year-old child presents with undescended testes as an isolated finding. If uncorrected, the patient might be expected to develop what complication?

*Your Own Answer*_____

Correct Answers

A556

The M-cells function as antigen-presenting cells.

A557

Stable cells are cells that normally are not dividing or have low levels of replication, but given the appropriate stimulus, can be capable of rapid proliferation. They include mesenchymal cells such as fibroblasts, osteoblasts, chondroblasts, and smooth muscle cells, as well as glandular parenchymal cells of the liver, kidney, and pancreas.

A558

Testicular cancer is a recognized complication of undescended testes. Impaired fertility can also result.

Questions

Q559

What are the beliefs regarding chromosomes and neoplasia as outlined by the Boveri hypothesis?

*Your Own Answer*_____

Q560

What is the infectious agent implicated in the development of cervical cancer?

*Your Own Answer*_____

Q561

What structure is located within the epidermis?

*Your Own Answer*_____

Correct Answers

A559

The Boveri hypothesis of 1914 on chromosomes and neoplasia maintained the belief that malignant cells are derived from normal cells, each tumor originates from a single cell, malignant cells have abnormal chromatin content, the tumor cell has lost the properties of a normal cell, and the cause of tumors is within the cell itself.

A560

Human papilloma virus, which causes venereal warts, is implicated in the development of cervical cancer.

A561

Free nerve endings are located in the epidermis and supply it with sensory innervation (i.e., pain, touch sensation).

Questions

Q562

The inguinal ligament is continuous inferiorly with which structure of the thigh?

*Your Own Answer*_____

Q563

What anti-acne agent has pseudotumor cerebri as a rare side effect?

*Your Own Answer*_____

Q564

In a population at equilibrium, three genotypes are present in the following proportions: A/A 0.81, a/a 0.01, where A and a are two alleles of a certain gene. What is the frequency of allele a in the population?

*Your Own Answer*_____

Correct Answers

A562

The inguinal ligament is a thickening of the external oblique aponeurosis, and is continuous with the deep fascia of the thigh, or fascia lata.

A563

Even though it is rare, there are documented cases of pseudotumor cerebri caused by Accutane.

A564

For an equilibrium population with two alleles A and a, the genotype frequencies are given by the Hardy-Weinberg Law: $(A + a)^2 = A^2 + 2Aa + a^2 = 1$ where A^2 is the frequency of the A/A homozygote; $2Aa$ is the frequency of the A/a heterozygote; and a^2 is the frequency of the a/a homozygote. Therefore, $a^2 = 0.1$, so $a = 0.1$.

Questions

Q565

What organ exhibits periarterial lymphatic sheaths?

*Your Own Answer*_____

Q566

A barium swallow study shows displacement of the esophagus. Distention of what cardiovascular structure is the most likely to be responsible?

*Your Own Answer*_____

Q567

What diagnostic test is used to test vitamin B12 absorption?

*Your Own Answer*_____

Correct Answers

A565

Periarterial lymphatic sheaths are a unique feature of the spleen.

A566

The left atrium lies in direct contact with the esophagus, and its distention is most likely responsible for the esophageal displacement.

A567

The Schilling test is used to measure the absorption of vitamin B12 in the presence and the absence of exogenous intrinsic factor.

Questions

Q568

What disease is a neoplasm of lymphocytes involving T-helper cells?

*Your Own Answer*_____

Q569

A 63-year-old male presents with signs of liver disease. Hepatitis screens are negative as is history for alcohol or other risk factors. Liver biopsy shows positive stain for excess iron. What is the most likely diagnosis?

*Your Own Answer*_____

Q570

What is the genetic transmission of Marfan's syndrome?

*Your Own Answer*_____

Correct Answers

A568

Mycosis fungoides is caused by T-helper lymphocytes, which infiltrate the skin, and results in a neoplasm of lymphocytes.

A569

Hemochromatosis is characterized by abnormally high levels of iron and liver damage with excessively high hepatic iron levels.

A570

Marfan's syndrome is autosomal dominant. Marfan's syndrome presents with skeletal abnormalities, such as excessive length of extremities, loose joints, kyphoscoliosis, and cardiovascular abnormalities, such as aortic aneurysm.

Questions

Granulomas are composed of activated macrophages. By what term are these known?

*Your Own Answer*_____

Which organism causes pneumonia and may be found colonizing air-conditioning systems?

*Your Own Answer*_____

Etretinate is a derivative of which vitamin?

*Your Own Answer*_____

Correct Answers

A571

Granulomas serve to isolate the focus of injury or infection. Granulomas are composed of activated macrophages, called epithelioid cells, which are organized into nodular aggregates. Also, cytoplasmically fused macrophages, or multinucleated giant cells, may be present.

A572

Legionella pneumophila is named after the first outbreak of Legionnaire's Disease in Philadelphia in 1976. In addition to pneumonia, patients may demonstrate an altered mental state.

A573

Etretinate is a vitamin A derivative, which is used in different skin diseases. Etretinate stays in the system for long periods of time, therefore, Etretinate should not be used in females of childbearing age.

Questions

Q574

A 32-year-old accountant rushes to the emergency room complaining of an unsubsidable erection. Past medical history of the patient reveals that he is being treated for depression. Which of the following is the most likely pharmacologic agent that was prescribed for his depressive state?

*Your Own Answer*_____

Q575

Multinuclear giant cells, seen in many pathological conditions, are formed by what type of fusion?

*Your Own Answer*_____

Q576

What deep fungus is capsulated?

*Your Own Answer*_____

Correct Answers

A574

Trazadone is the most likely pharmacologic agent.

A575

Macrophages fuse in certain pathological conditions to form multinucleated giant cells.

A576

The only truly capsulated deep fungus is cryptococcus. Even though histoplasmosis is called histoplasma capsulatum, it does not truly possess a capsule.

Questions

Q577

An inhaled object coming in contact with the carina elicits a substantial cough reflex. What would carry the afferent limb of this reflex?

*Your Own Answer*_____

Q578

Your patient has a tumor of gastrin-producing enteroendocrine cells (G-cells). Anatomically, where is the tumor most likely located?

*Your Own Answer*_____

Q579

A stab wound to the chest has resulted in a small tear in the aorta, near the ligamentum arteriosum. The aortic tear was repaired surgically and the patient survived. On the next day, the patient exhibited hoarseness. What is the most likely explanation?

*Your Own Answer*_____

Correct Answers

A577

The vagus nerve supplies sensory innervation to the carina and would mediate the cough reflex.

A578

Enteroendocrine cells that secrete gastrin (G-cells) are located in the glands of the pyloric region of the stomach.

A579

The recurrent laryngeal nerve was likely damaged by the knife, or during surgery, since the nerve crosses the aorta just medial to the ligamentum arteriosum. Damage to this nerve unilaterally would cause hoarseness.

Questions

Q580

What are the cutaneous manifestations of rheumatic fever?

*Your Own Answer*_____

Q581

A patient who excludes the vegetable-fruit food group from his diet will most likely develop a deficiency of which vitamin?

*Your Own Answer*_____

Q582

What cellular event is most central to the development of irreversible cellular injury?

*Your Own Answer*_____

Correct Answers

A580

The cutaneous manifestations of rheumatic fever include subcutaneous nodules, erythema marginatum, and erythema papulatum. Subcutaneous nodules usually are seen on the bony prominences.

A581

Vitamin A comes in two types: provitamin A from plants and performed vitamin A from animal sources. The major provitamin A is B-carotene and is found in yellow and orange vegetables. The main source of performed vitamin A are from liver, milk, fish oil, and eggs. Lack of vegetables can cause vitamin A deficiency.

A582

Cellular injury is associated with changes that are reversible and irreversible and which may lead to necrosis, or cell death. Rupture of the plasma and mitochondrial membranes is associated with irreversible cell injury.

Questions

Q583

The pituitary fossa lies directly posterior and superior to which structure?

*Your Own Answer*_____

Q584

Which drug used in the treatment of tuberculosis has reversible liver injury as a complication of treatment?

*Your Own Answer*_____

Q585

In a lung biopsy, how would Type I alveolar cells differ from Type II alveolar cells ?

*Your Own Answer*_____

Correct Answers

A583

The sphenoid sinus is anatomically related to the pituitary fossa.

A584

Isoniazid causes serious but reversible liver injury in a small percentage of patients.

A585

Type II cells contain lipid-rich (dipalmitoyl lecithin) cytoplasmic granules, which, upon exocytosis, will contribute to the surfactant lining the surface. Type I cells do not contain these granules.

Questions

Q586

What is the most important agent in promoting the degranulation of mast cells?

*Your Own Answer*_____

Q587

Operative risk for patients undergoing shunting procedures for portal hypertension can be best assessed by what classification system?

*Your Own Answer*_____

Q588

A patient with elevated blood levels of insulin and glucagon was diagnosed as having a tumor at which site?

*Your Own Answer*_____

Correct Answers

A586

Il-1 is the most important agent that promotes degranulation of mast cells. Il-1 promotes mast cells to release chemical mediaters, such as histamine.

A587

The Child classification uses serum bilirubin, serum albumin, and presence of ascites, encephalopathy, and malnutrition to determine operative risk for patients undergoing shunting procedures.

A588

A tumor of the pancreas would be diagnosed, because insulin and glucagon are produced by cells of the islets of Langerhans in the pancreas.

Questions

Q589

Compare healing by secondary intention to healing by first intention.

*Your Own Answer*_____

Q590

Psuedomembranous colitis is usually caused by toxins of which *Clostridium* bacteria?

*Your Own Answer*_____

Q591

What is the typical location for necrobiosis lipoidica diabeticorum?

*Your Own Answer*_____

Correct Answers

A589

Granulation tissue is present in both healing by secondary intention and healing by primary intention. Secondary union is characterized by a more intense inflammatory reaction, including more necrotic debris, inflammatory exudate, and fibrin. Wound contracture is also seen in secondary intention, but not in first intention.

A590

Clostridium dificile produces toxin A, an enterotoxin, and toxin B, which causes certain cytopathic effects in cultured cells. *C. dificile* colitis often occurs after a course of broad-spectrum antibiotics, *C perfringens* causes an anaerobic cellulitis/myonecrosis, or gas gangrene, *C botulinum* causes botulism, and *C tetani* causes tetanus.

A591

Necrobiosis lipoidica diabeticorum is a condition for which one or more shiny lesions usually develop on the anterior lower legs. It is related to diabetes.

Questions

Q592

Calorie and protein malnutrition in an otherwise healthy person is referred to by what term?

*Your Own Answer*_____

Q593

Patients with erythromelagia have what change in their skin temperature?

*Your Own Answer*_____

Q594

A 54-year-old female is taking procainamide for her cardiac condition. Eight months later, she develops arthralgias, rash, myalgias, and a pleural effusion. She was found to have a fever of 101°. What antibody titer would be positive in this particular condition?

*Your Own Answer*_____

Correct Answers

A592

Marasmus is deficiency of a wide range of nutrients, including carbohydrates and protein. Kwashiorkor refers to protein deficiency in the setting of adequate caloric intake.

A593

Erythromelalgia (Gerhardt's or Mitchell's disease) presents with increased blood flow and large pulses, as well as an increase in the skin temperature.

A594

Anti-histone antibody is associated with drug-induced lupus. This syndrome develops in approximately 15–20% of patients receiving hydralazine or procainamide. Nephritis or CNS involvement is not typical in this syndrome.

Questions

Q595

What is the most common cause of hyperthyroidism?

*Your Own Answer*_____

Q596

What melanoma is more common in non-Caucasian populations?

*Your Own Answer*_____

Q597

In a severe case of anterior compartment syndrome, what structures would be vulnerable to compression due to the increased pressure within this tight fascial compartment?

*Your Own Answer*_____

Correct Answers

A595

Graves' disease (diffuse toxic goiter) is the most common cause of hyperthyroidism. It is an autoimmune condition in which antibodies stimulate the gland.

A596

Malignant melanoma is one of the most dangerous skin cancers that is usually seen in the Caucasian population. However, acral lentiginous malignant melanoma is more common in the non-Caucasian population.

A597

The anterior tibial artery and deep peroneal nerve lie in the anterior compartment of the leg, and are vulnerable in prolonged anterior compartment syndrome.

Questions

Q598

What compound is an antagonist of heparin?

*Your Own Answer*_____

Q599

What type of radiation is used to treat mycoses fungoides?

*Your Own Answer*_____

Q600

What are the common cutaneous symptoms of hepatitis B?

*Your Own Answer*_____

Correct Answers

A598

Protamine, a strongly basic compound, antagonizes the negatively charged heparin. 1mg of protamine will antagonize about 100 units of heparin.

A599

Cutaneous T-cell lymphoma, which is also known as mycosis fungoidis, is a disorder of the lymphocytes. There is no good treatment for this condition. However, different treatment modalities, including light treatment, such as UVB and PUVA, photophoresis, are all used.

A600

The most common cutaneous manifestations of hepatitis B are urticaria, polyarteritis nodosa, and cryoglobulinemia, in addition to Gianotti-Crosti syndrome, which is erythematous papules and vesicles on the distal extremities (usually seen in children).

Questions

Q601

What are the risk factors for colorectal cancer?

*Your Own Answer*_____

Q602

Reperfusion of myocardial infarcts are associated with what types of injury changes?

*Your Own Answer*_____

Q603

Patients may present as pale (anemic) or hemorrhagic when they are infarcted. What factor predisposes an individual to anemia as opposed to hemorrhage?

*Your Own Answer*_____

Correct Answers

A601

Patients at risk for breast cancer and ovarian cancer are at risk for colorectal cancer. Two first-degree relatives with colorectal cancer is a risk factor. Inflammatory bowel disease, such as ulcerative colitis, is a risk factor.

A602

Myocardial infarcts that are subendocardial or non-transmural are often caused by diffuse myocardial ischemia and often show reperfusion injury changes. These changes include contraction band necrosis and hemorrhage.

A603

Hemorrhagic infarction is characterized by spongy tissue density, dual or collateral circulation, venous occlusion, and reperfusion. Arterial occlusion predisposes an individual to anemic infarction and is characterized by solid tissue density.

BLANK CARDS
To Make Up
Your Own Questions

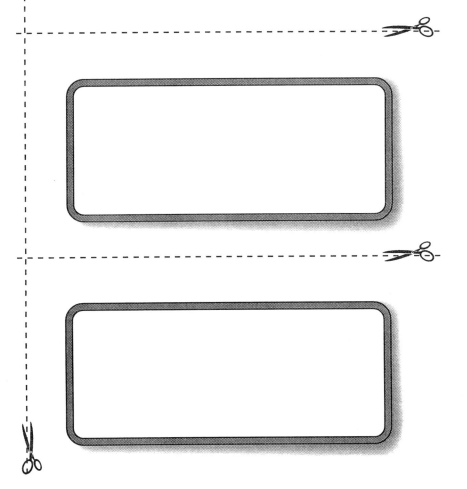

CORRECT ANSWERS

for

Your Own Questions

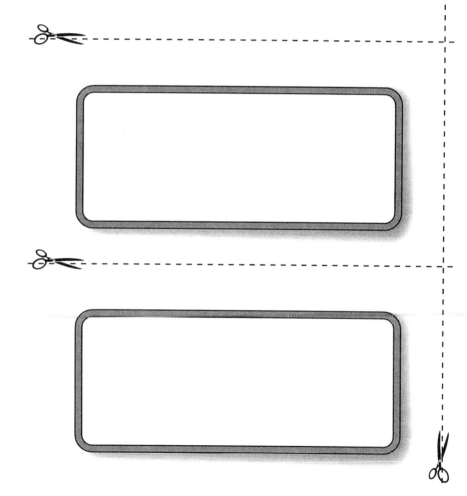

Blank Cards for
Your Own Questions

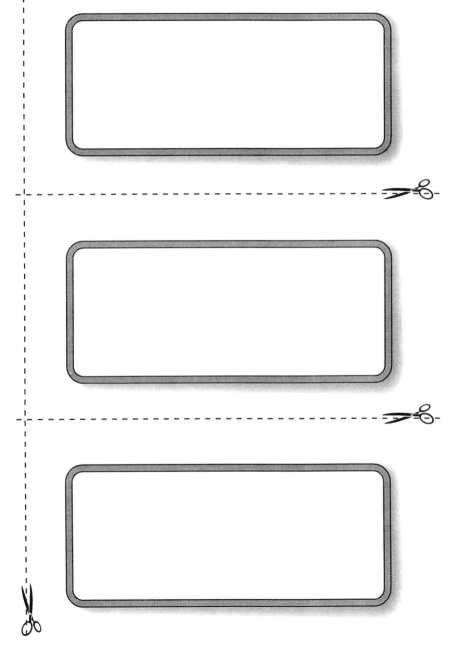

Correct Answers

Blank Cards for *Your Own Questions*

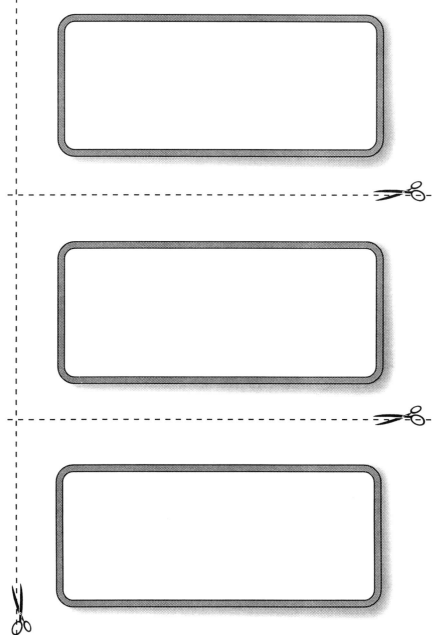

Correct Answers

Blank Cards for
Your Own Questions

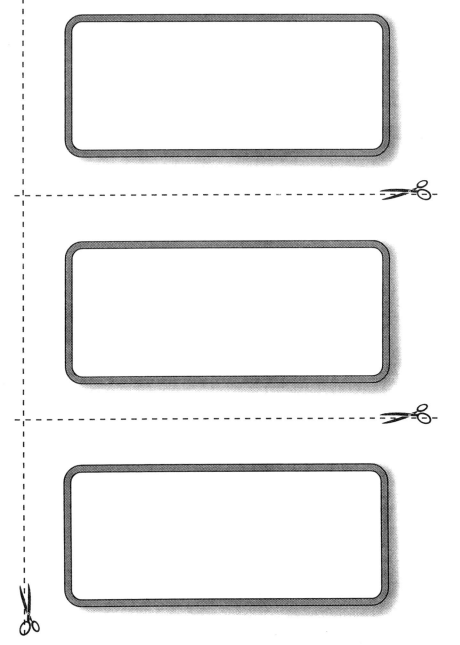

Correct Answers

Blank Cards for
Your Own Questions

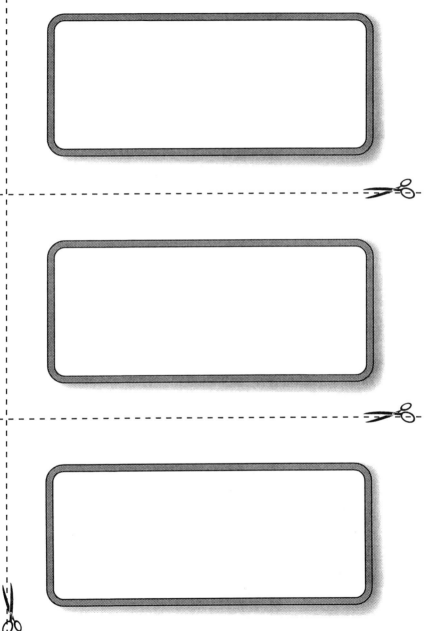

Correct Answers

Blank Cards for
Your Own Questions

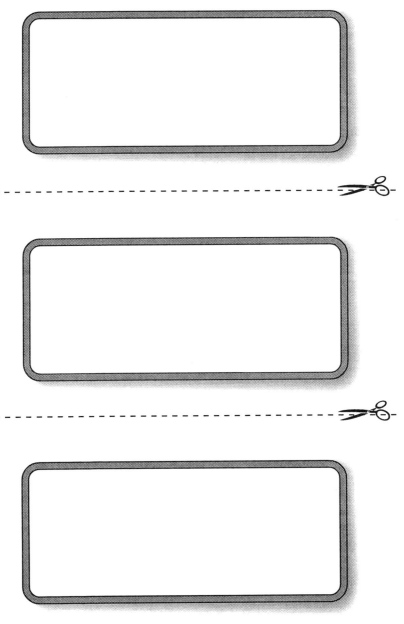

Correct Answers

Blank Cards for
Your Own Questions

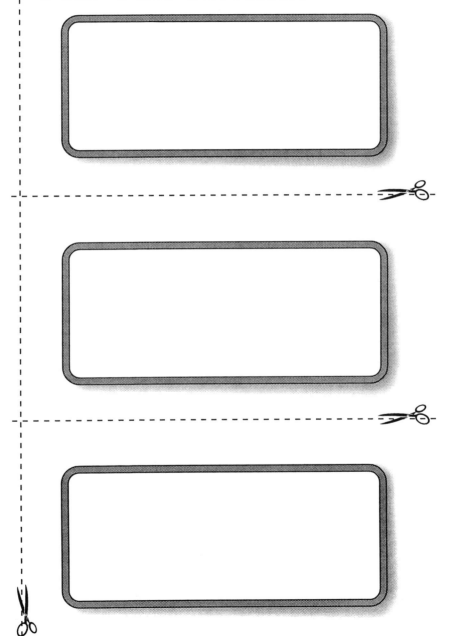

Correct Answers

Blank Cards for
Your Own Questions

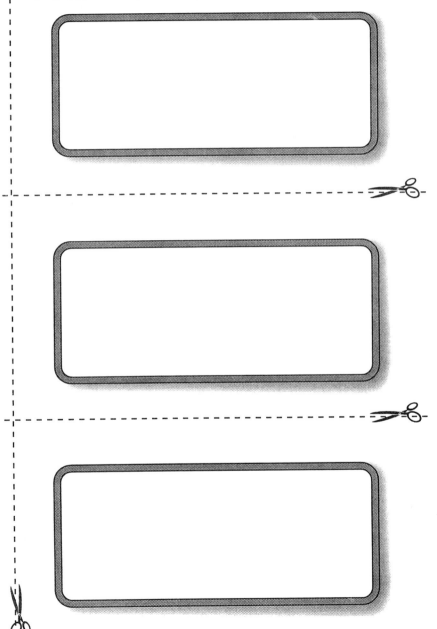

Correct Answers

Blank Cards for
Your Own Questions

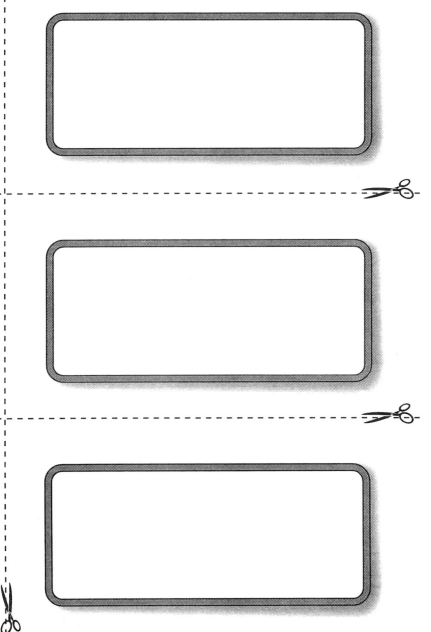

Correct Answers

Blank Cards for
Your Own Questions

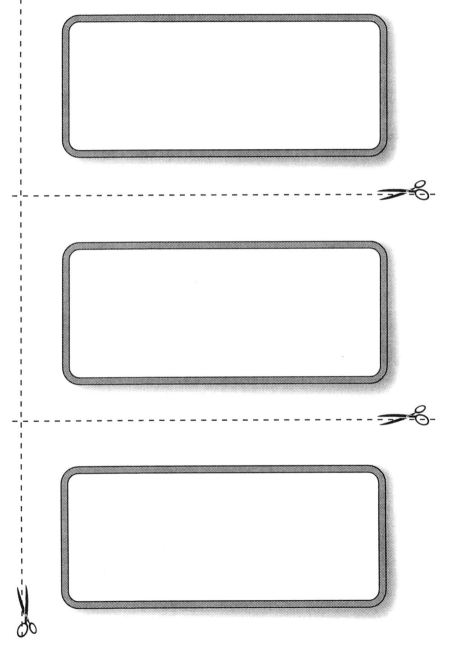

Correct Answers

Blank Cards for
Your Own Questions

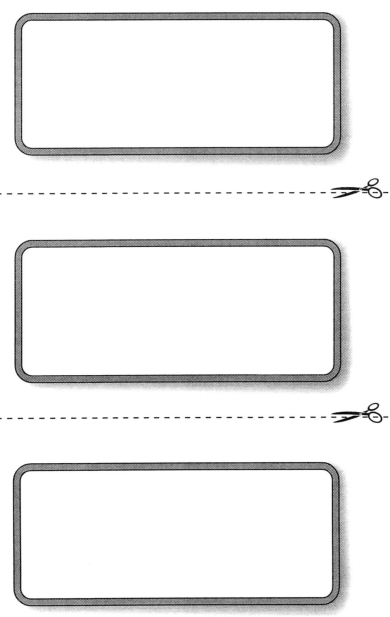

Correct Answers

Blank Cards for
Your Own Questions

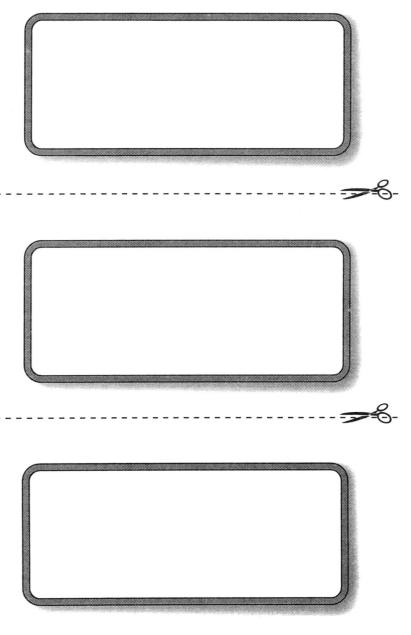

Correct Answers

Blank Cards for
Your Own Questions

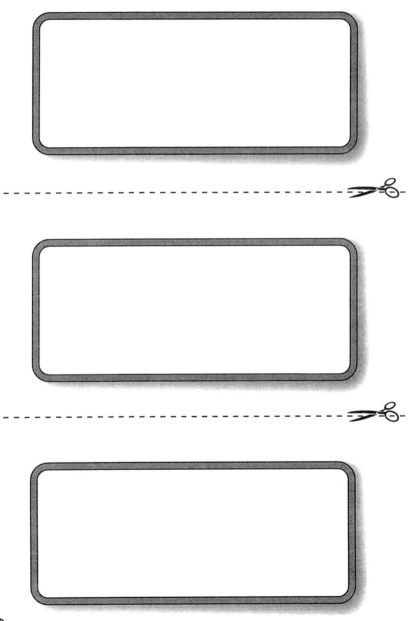

Correct Answers

Blank Cards for
Your Own Questions

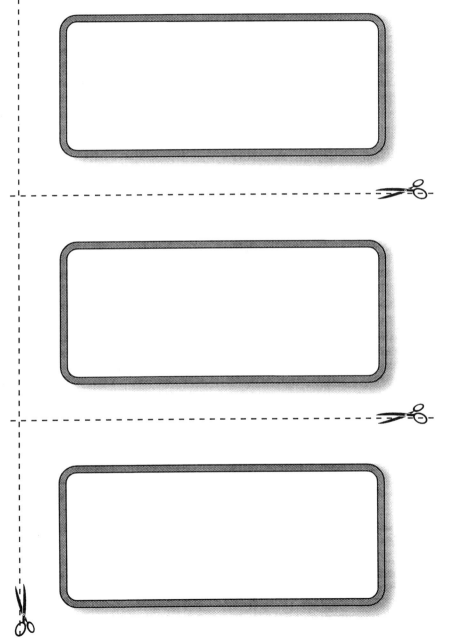

Correct Answers

Blank Cards for
Your Own Questions

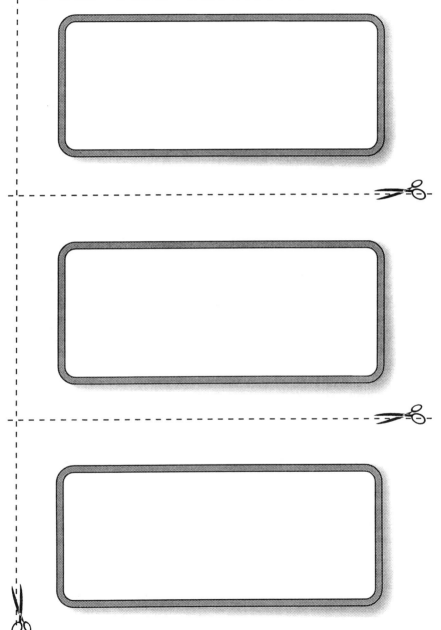

Correct Answers

Blank Cards for
Your Own Questions

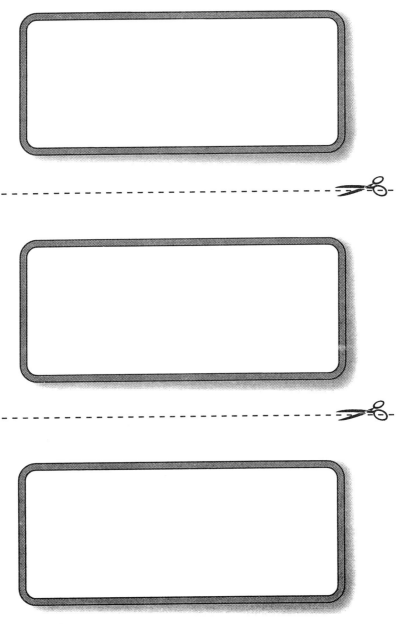

Correct Answers

Blank Cards for
Your Own Questions

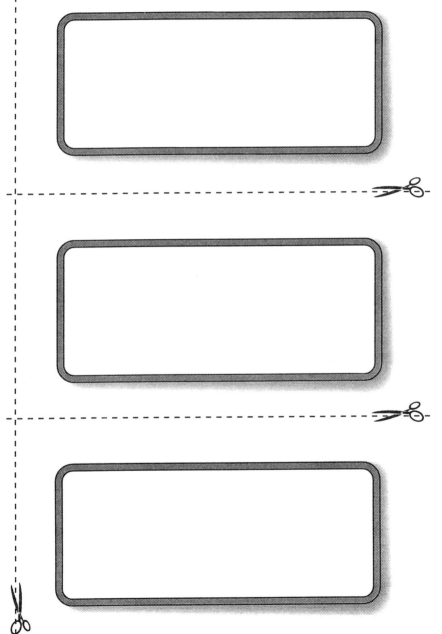

Correct Answers

Blank Cards for
Your Own Questions

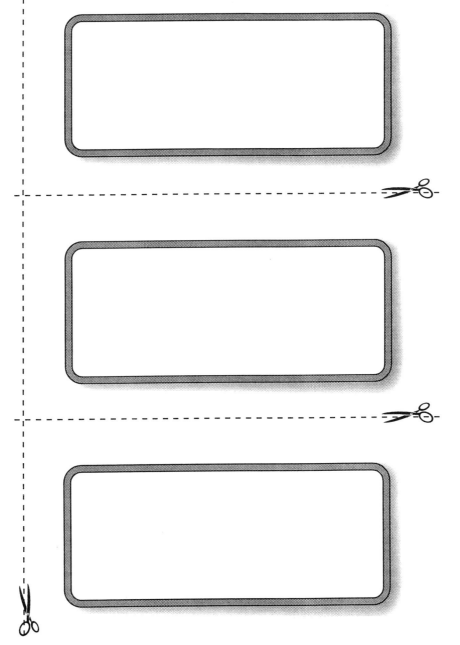

Correct Answers

Blank Cards for
Your Own Questions

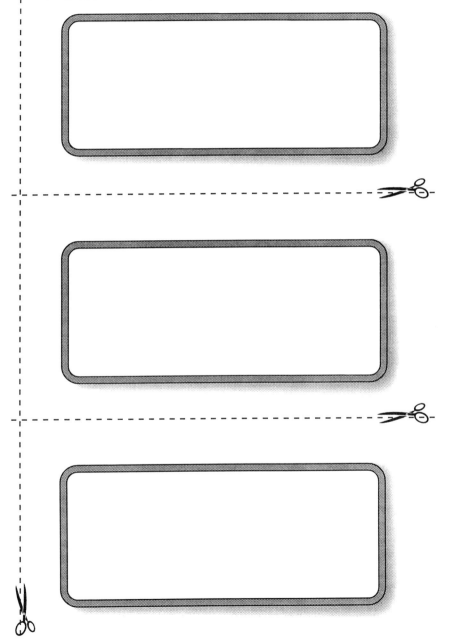

Correct Answers

Blank Cards for
Your Own Questions

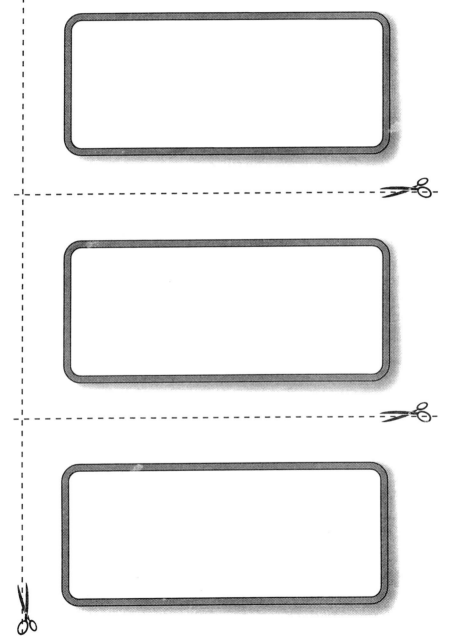

Correct Answers

INDEX

Note: Numbers in the Index refer to question numbers.

Abdomen:
  intraabdominal abscess, 109
  wounds, 494
Abdominal arteries, 462
Abdominal cavity, 466
Abdominal fascia, 320
Abdominal pain, 50, 393, 446, 502
Abdominal wall, surgical incision
  into, 164
Abortion, spontaneous, 380
Acarbose, 540
Accutane, 203
  side effects of, 563
Acetylcholine, 502
  enzymes that hydrolyze, 56
Acetylcholinesterase, 119
Acne, 536
  cystic, 203
  treatment of, 562
Acrodermatitis enterohepatica, 470
Acute-phase reaction, 381, 413
Addison's disease, 342
Adenocarcinoma, 395
Adenomatous polyposis coli (APC)
  gene, 95
Adenopathy, 70
Adipose tissue, 320
Adrenal cortex, 160, 337, 520
Adrenal glands, 42, 337
Adrenal mass, incidental, 42
Adrenal medulla, 440, 499
Adrenal tumors, 42, 440, 520
  cancer, 42
Adrenal veins, left, 250
Aflatoxin, 316
Agammaglobulinemia, X-linked, 36
Aganglionic region, 38
Agoraphobia, 398

AIDS patients, 293
  anal lesions in, 148
  cause of retinitis in, 280
  infections in, 121, 124
Air-conditioning systems,
  colonizing:
  organisms in, 572
Al-antitrypsin, 498
Albinism, 19, 103
Albumin, 381
Alcock's canal. See Pudendal canal
Alkaptonuria, 110, 550
Alleles of genes, 14
Allergic hypersensitivity, 344
Allergic reactions, 106, 276, 392
Alpha fetoprotein, in amniotic fluid,
  82
Alveolar capillary endothelial cells,
  46
Alveolar cells, 429, 585
Alveolar macrophages, 525
Alveolar wall, 46
  elastic fibers in, 372
Alzheimer's disease:
  cerebral neurons in, 31
  treatment, 251
Amino acids, 313
Aminoglycosides, blood levels of, 434
Amniotic fluid, 82
Amyloid, 332
Anaerobic pathogens, 109
Anal-receptive intercourse, 148
Anaphylaxis, 392, 404
Anasarca, 40
Androstenedione, 111
Anemia, 300, 393
  predisposing factors, 603
Anencephaly, 82
Aneurysms, 49, 152, 169, 187, 233,
  503
Angioimmunoblastic
  lymphadenopathy, 228
Angiomas, spider, 37

Anterior compartment syndrome, 597
Antiarrhythmic drugs, side effects of, 93
Antibiotics, 112
    penicillin class, 167
Antibodies, 44, 168, 219, 261, 326, 382, 404, 594
Anticholinergic agents, 4
Anticholinesterase inhibitors, 56
Anticoagulants, 155
Anticonvulsants, side effects of, 107
Antifungal drugs, 450
Antihistamines, side effects of, 511
Anti-histone antibody, 594
Antineutrophil autoantibodies (ANCAs), 166
Aorta, 441
    tears of, 579
Aortic aneurysm, 503
Aortic dissection, 49
APC mutations, 95
Aponeurosis, external oblique, 555, 562
Appendicitis, symptoms of, 172
Appendix, 149, 172
Argyll-Robertson pupil, 191
Aromatic amine exposure, 285
Arteries, 2, 88, 151, 152, 166, 169, 331, 365, 462
    coronary, 156, 457, 509
    microanatomy, 357
    occlusion, 54
    thyroid, 252, 278
Arterioles, 321
    neurogenic vasoconstriction of, 467
Arteriosus, patent ductus, 439
Arteriovenous malformation, 216
Arteritis, 227
    polyarteritis, 75, 166
Arthritis, 30, 118, 354

psoriatic, 419
rheumatoid, 100
Asbestos, 201
Aspergillus fumigatus, 143
Aspirin, 174, 329
Asthma, 143
Ataxia-telangiectasia, 184, 317
Atherosclerosis, 169, 187, 189, 260
    risk factors, 451
Atrium, 566
Atropine, 56
Auto-antibodies, 299, 387
Autoimmune diseases, 281, 355, 541. See also specific diseases
Autosomal diseases, 19, 184, 206, 305, 317, 322, 366, 380, 470, 539
Axonal hyperplasia, 32
Azelaic acid, 323
Bacteria, 59, 192, 287, 328
    Gram-positive vs. Gram-negative, 22, 41, 193, 401, 449
    spread of, 537
Bacteroides species, 8
Barium swallow, 566
Barr body, 145
Bartonella henselae, 428
Basal cell carcinoma, 221
Basal ganglia lesions, 79
Basophilia, 476
B-cell counts, low, 36
Bechet's disease, 356
Bee stings, 392
Bell's palsy, 526
Beriberi, 154, 282, 359
Beta-lactamase, 167
Bezoars, treatment for, 324
Bile salts, 217
Bilirubin, increased unconjugated, 265
Bipolar disorder, drug treatment of, 425
Birbeck granules, 275

Black widow, 26
Bladder. See Urinary bladder
Bleeding disorders, 196
Blindness:
  night, 123
  river, 379
Blood, 237
  substance levels in, 434
  calcium, 3, 7, 32
  sugar, 190, 540
Blood coagulation, 108, 155, 158, 202
  anticoagulants, 155
  disseminated intravascular coagulopathy, 295
  hypercoagulability, 108, 158, 446
Blood-brain barrier, 46, 126, 247
Blood-nerve barrier, 286
Blood-thymus barrier, 16
Bone disease, 163, 210, 496
  cancer, 224
Bone formation and development, 9, 415
Bone fractures, 244
Bone marrow cells, in Hodgkin's disease, 396
Bone marrow platelets, 162
Borderline personality disorder, 473
Botryomycosis, 57
Botulism, 502
Boveri hypothesis, 559
Bowel disease, 38, 134
  inflammatory, 601
Bowel flora, 112
Bowman's glands, 81
Brain. See also Pituitary gland
  adrenal cortex, 160, 337, 520
  adrenal medulla, 440, 499
  medulla, 405
Brain tumors, 160
Breast cancer, 243, 601
  metastasis of, 435

risk factors for, 15
Bronchiole, 390
Bronchitis, in infants, 36
Bronchopulmonary lymph nodes, 277
Bronchus, 458
  segmental, 390
Brunner's glands, 258
Budd-Chiari syndrome, 446
Buerger's disease, 227
Bulbospongiosus muscle, 345
Bullae, 353
Bullous disease, primary, 535
Burns, 1st vs. 2nd vs. 3rd degree, 273
C5a, 60
Café au-lait macules, 19
Calcification, 12
Calcinosis, in children, 75
Calcium, 358
  blood levels, 3, 7, 32
Calorie deficiency, 592
Cancer, 43, 104, 433, 601. See also Carcinoma; Leukemia; Sarcoma; Skin diseases, cancer
  adrenal, 42
  bladder, 285, 552
  bone, 224
  brain, 42
  breast, 15, 243, 435, 601
  cervical, 559
  colon, 24
  colorectal, 601
  diethylstilbestrol and, 395
  Down's syndrome and, 133
  esophageal, 456
  hepatic, 316
  HIV infection and, 64
  liver, 459
  lung, 528
  migratory thrombophlebitis and, 45

nonmetastic, 221
oral, 490
ovarian, 367, 529, 601
parotid gland, 351
peanuts and, 316
prostate, 255, 267
scrotum, 491
sex differences in incidence of, 348
soft tissue, 256
spread through lymph nodes, 6, 367
tongue, 29
in women, 350
Capillaries, of blood-brain barrier, 247
Caput medusae, 452
Carbon monoxide poisoning, 127, 150
Carbon tetrachloride, 20
Carboxyhemoglobin level, 127
Carcinoid tumors, in liver, 459
Carcinoma, 395
  basal cell, 221
  colon, 318
  duodenal, 74
  lung, 43
  medullary, 243
Cardiac antiarrhythmic drugs, 120
Cardiac arrhythmia, 425
Cardiac murmurs, 72
Cardiac muscle, 505. See also Myocardial infarction
Cardiovascular risk factors, 181
Carina, 577
Carotid arteries, internal, 88
Carotid body, 237
Cartilage disease, 299
Catalase, organisms lacking, 389
Cat-scratch disease, etiology of, 428
Cavernous sinus, 445
Cells:

multinuclear giant, 575
  stable, 557
Cellular injury, 582
Cell-wall synthesis, 287
Central nervous system, radiosensitivity of, 34
Cerebral infarction, 94
Cerebrospinal fluid, 480
Cervical cancer, 559
Cervical mucus, 453
Chagas' disease, 70
Chediak-Higashi syndrome, 19
Chemotactic factors, 60
Chest pain, 174
"Chest tap," 141
Chest wounds, 178
Child classification, 587
Childbirth, 345
Chlamydia trachomatis, 91
Chloramphenicol, side effects in neonates of, 302
Chloroquine, 211, 465
Cholesterol, 217
  HDL vs. LDL, 438
Cholinesterase inhibitors, 251
Chondrodermatitis nodularis helicis, 378
Choristoma, 87
Choroid plexus tumor, 480
Chromaffin cells, 42
Chromaffin tumor, 440
Chromatids, 283
Chromatin, 476
Chromosome instability syndromes, 304
Chromosomes:
  neoplasia and, 559
  translocation of, 104, 153
  X
  diseases linked to, 146
  in females, 486
  inactivation, 145

Cinchonism, drug-induced, 93
Cirrhosis:
    causes, 37
    primary biliary, 406
Clonorchis sinensis, 508
Clostridium, 41, 59
Clostridium difficile, 112
Coagulation. See Blood coagulation
Coblet cells, 291
Cocci, Gram-positive, 22, 449
Coccidioidomycosis, 230
Colchicine, side effects of, 363
Colitis, 112, 590
Collagen fibers, 12, 447
Colliculi, inferior, 199
Colon, bacteria in, 8
Colon disease, 38, 95
    cancer, 24, 318, 601
Colonic polyps, 95
Colorectal cancer, 601
Comedones, 536
Condyloma acuminata, 485
Conjunctivitis, 30
    infectious neonatal, 91
Contraceptives, oral, 116, 346
Coomb's test, 44
Copper, accumulation of, 37
Coronary arteries, 509
Coronary artery by-pass graft
    (CABG), 457
Coronary sinus, 220
Corpus luteum, 533
    degeneration of, 31
Corticospinal tract, lateral, 204
Corynebacteria, 192
Corynebacterium minutissumum,
    328
Costal pleura, 376
Cough reflex, 577
Coughing, dry, 114
Cpk, 174
Cranial nerve, 526

Creeping eruption, 55
Cremaster muscle, 410
CREST syndrome, 208
Crohn's disease, 132
Cruciate ligament, posterior, 66
Cryptococcal meningitis, 124
Cryptococcosis, 73
Cryptococcus, 73
C-sis, 105
Culdocentesis, 51
Curschmann's spirals, 143
Cyanide poisoning, 368
Cyclosporine, 177, 297
Cystic acne, 203
Cystic fibrosis, 206, 305
Cystic medial necrosis, 49
Cysts, 122, 210
Cytomegalovirus (CMV), 35, 148,
    280
Cytotoxic response, 128
Dapsone, 161
    indications for, 417
    side effects, 402
DDC mutations, 95
Deafness, 199
Death, leading causes of, 517
Deep venous thromboses (DVTs),
    346
Dehydration, 50
Dehydroepiandrosterone
    production, 160
Delusions of parasitosis, drug
    treatment for, 497
Dendritic hypertrophy, 32
Dentate line, 84
Depression, 28
Dermal papillae, 239
Dermatitis:
    causes, 1
    in children, 75
    seborrheic, 147
Dermatitis herpetiformis, 161

Dermatological symptoms, 19, 21,
    470, 535. See also Melanoma;
    Psoriasis; Skin diseases,
    cancer
Dermatomes, 12
Dermatomyositis, 388
    juvenile, 75
    muscles affected in, 15
Detrusor muscle, 314
Diabetes, 12, 181, 307
    complications of, 547, 591
Diarrhea, 426
    watery, 50
Diet, 581
Diethylstilbestrol (DES), utero
    exposure to, 395
Digoxin, 411
Dilantin, 382
Disk spaces, intervertebral:
    radiodensity, 110
Disseminated intravascular
    coagulopathy (DIC), 295
Diuresis, 11
Diverticulosis, 551
DNA, 115, 283, 553
DNA fragments, 257
DNA helicase gene, 532
DNA synthesis, 214
Dovonex, 112
Down's syndrome, 82, 96, 133
Ductal hyperplasia, 116
Ductus venosus, 197
Duodenal ulcers, 325
Duodenum, 25, 455
    Brunner's glands in, 258
Dyspareunia, female, 102
Dysphagia, 455
Dysplastic nevi, 420
Ecchymosis, 423
Echinococcosis, 122
Echtyma, 469
Edema, 21

causes of, 500
    types of, 40
EKG, 174, 188
Emboli, sources of, 94
Embolism, types of, 158
Embryonic yolk stalk, persistence of
    remnant, 71
Emphysema, 240
Endocarditis, 72, 176
Endometriosis, 102
Endometrium growth, 504
Endoplasmic reticulum,
    endoplasmic, 131
Endothelial cells, 46
Endothelial damage, 108, 158, 189
Enteritis, 198
Enterobiasis, drugs used to treat, 63
Enterocolitis, 112
Enzyme deficiencies, 454
Enzymes, hydrolyzing, 56
Eosinophil count, 55
Eosinophilia, 143
Eosinophilic granuloma, 224
Eosinophils, 106
Epidermal necrolysis, toxic, 215, 262
Epidermis, 157, 546, 561
    sweat duct obstruction in, 90
Epiglottitis, in children, 231
Epileptic seizures, 460
Epinephrine, 440
Episiotomy, mediolateral, 345
Epithelial cells, 58, 424
Epithelial chloride transport, 206
Epithelium, 556
Epstein-Barr virus, 35, 69, 142, 153,
    487
Erection, unsubsidable, 574
Erysipeloid, 506
Erysipelothrix rhusiopathiae, 506
Erythema ab igne, 53
Erythema nodosum, 186
Erythematous nodules, 186

Erythematous papules, 65
Erythematous plaque on elbow, 118
Erythematous rash, 215
Erythrasma, 192, 328
Erythromelalgia, 593
Erythropoietin, 135
Escherichia coli, 198
Esophageal cancer, 456
Esophageal varices, 452
Esophagus, 178, 364
    displacement of, 566
Estradiol secretion, 504
Estrogen levels, in menopause, 28
Ethambutol, side effects, 246
Ethosuximide, 460
Etretinate, 573
Excision repair pathway, 242
Eyes, damage to, 330
Facial eruptions, 179
Factor VIII protein, 269
Falx inguinalis, 241
Fascia, 17, 18, 311, 320, 494
    types of, 164
Fascia lata, 17
Fascicles, 263
Femoral canal, 270
Fenton Reaction, 52
Fertility, impaired, 558
Fetoprotein, 82
Fibrillin genes, 49
    defective, 49
Fibrin platelet embolization, 94
Fibrinoid necrosis, 166, 169
Fibroblasts, 12, 447
Fistula, 132
Flaccid bullae, 535
Follicle-stimulating hormone, 28
Follicular cells, 472
Foot movement, constriction in,
    545
Foot tendons, 513
Fox-Fordyce disease, 207

Freckling, axillary, 19
Fungi, 73, 124, 409, 599
    encapsulated, 576
    spore size, 230
Furosemide, side effects of, 11
Gangrenosum, pyoderma, 134
Gardner's syndrome, 306
Gastric artery, 364
Gastric lumen, hair in, 386
Gastric tumors, 482
Gastrin production, excessive, 482
Gastrin-producing enteroendocrine
    cells (G-cells):
    tumors of, 577
Gastroesophageal junction, 361
Gastroparesis, diagnostic testing
    for, 77
Gaucher's disease, 519
Genes, 95, 254, 532
    alleles of, 14
    fibrillin, 49
    HPRT, 442
Genetic transmission, 343
Genital warts, 485
Genitofemoral nerve, 410
Genotypes, 14, 461, 564
Gianotti-Crosti syndrome, 65
Gilbert's syndrome, 265
Gingival hyperplasia, 107
Glomerulonephritis, in children, 75
Glucagon levels, elevated, 588
Glucose-6–phosphate
    dehydrogenase deficiency,
    300
Gluteus maximus, 17
Gold, 211
Gout, 310
    conditions causing
        predisposition to, 80
    correlates and symptoms of, 80
Graft rejection cells, 97
Gram stain, 59

Gram-positive vs. Gram-negative
    bacteria, 22, 41, 193, 401, 449
Granulation tissue, 589
Granuloma, 138, 224, 571
Granuloma annulare, 547
Granulomatous inflammation,
    causes of, 245
Granulosa cells of ovarian follicles,
    111
Granulosa lutein cells, 173
Gray baby syndrome, 302
Griseofulvin, 450
Growth factor, 105
Gums, hyperplasia of, 107
Gyrus, precentral, 384
H. influenzae, 371
Hailey-Hailey disease, 539
Hair in gastric lumen, 386
Hamartoma, 87
Hamartomatous polyps of
    intestines, 74
Hansen's disease, 341
Hardy-Weinberg Law, 14, 461
Hassal's corpuscles, 58
Hayflick limit, 67
Headaches, 42
Head-up tilt table testing, 444
Heart. See also Cardiac muscle;
    Myocardial infarction
    apex of, 159
    diaphragm and, 374
    ischemia in sinoatrial node, 54
    Purkinje fibers, 523
Heart failure, congestive:
    systolic dysfunction of ventricle
        in, 397
Heart injury, 220
Heart valves, 94
    calcification of, 399
Helicobacter pylori, 325
Hematopoietic system, 171
Hemiparesis, 176

Hemiparesis, left-sided, 94
Hemochromatosis, 569
Hemoglobin, 13, 127, 393, 402
Hemolytic-uremic syndrome, 198
Hemophilia, 269
Hemophilus influenzae b, 231
Hemoptysis, 114
Hemorrhage:
    due to warfarin, 427
    subcutaneous, 423
Hemorrhages, splinter, 72
Hemorrhagic infarction,
    predisposing factors, 603
Hemorrhagic necrosis of, 337
Hemorrhoids, 452
    internal vs. external, 84
Hemosiderin pigment, 525
Henoch-Schönlein purpura, 414
Heparin, 598
Hepatic cancer, 316, 459
Hepatic centrilobular necrosis, 20
Hepatic tumors, 346
Hepatitis, 65, 268, 468, 600
Hepatomegaly, 446
Hepatorenal recess, 5
Hernia:
    diaphragmatic, 292
    indirect inguinal, 222
    surgical repair of, 410
Herpes virus, 35
Herpetic ulcers, 148
Hindgut:
    nerves supplying, 510
Hirschprung's disease:
    cause, 38
Histamine, 344
Histamine release, 276
Histoplasmosis, 409
    diagnostic testing for, 549
HIV, 264
HIV infection, 69, 479
    cancer associated with, 64

HLA-B27, 281
Hoarseness, 579
Hodgkin's disease, bone marrow in, 396
lymphoma, 554
Homogentisic oxidase deficiency, 550
Hormones, 28, 32, 173, 217, 272
Horner's syndrome, 321, 330, 524
Hot flashes, 28
HPRT gene, 442
HPRT genes, 442
Hyaline deposits, 117, 430
Hyaline sclerosis, 169
Hydralazine, 382
Hypercalcuria, 512
Hypercoagulation of blood, 108, 158, 446
Hyperglycemia, 307
Hyperimmunoglobulinemia E recurrent infectious syndrome, 391
Hyperkeratosis, 30
Hyperketonemia, 307
Hyperkinesia, 79
Hyperlipoproteinemia I, 471
Hyperparathyroidism, 12
Hyperpigmentation, 315
Hyperpigmentation of skin and mucous membrane, 74
Hyperplasia of gums, 107
Hyperpnea, 303
Hypertension, 373, 451, 587
due to tumor, 520
Hyperthyroidism, 595
Hyperuricemia, 12
Hypoglycemia, 342
Hypogonadism, primary: characteristics, 407
Hypophyseal arteries, 88
Hypophyseal fossa, 23
Hypotension, orthostatic, 444
Hysterectomy, 515

IgA, 219, 414
IgE, 276
IgG, 261
IgG antibodies, 168
IgM, 326
Il-1, 586
Ilioinguinal nerve, 222
Iliotibial tract, 17
Immune cells, 260
Immune complexes, 166
Immune system:
impairments in, 387
Immunoglobulin:
abnormal monoclonal, 416
low levels of, 36, 276
Immunologic abnormalities, 184
Impetigo, 469
Impetigo herpetiformis, 530
Incontinence:
urinary, 4
Incontinenta pigmenti, 146
Infarctions, 94, 294, 346, 602, 603
myocardial, 174, 346, 517, 518
Infection:
post-venereal, 30
Inflammation, 21
acute
vascular changes in, 288
chronic vs. acute, 21
Infraorbital nerve:
damage to, 62
Infundibulopelvic ligament, 365
Inguinal canal, 222, 270
Inguinal hernia, 222
indirect, 33
in newborns, 33
Inguinal ligament, 555, 562
Inguinal nodes, 274
Inguinal tendon, 241
Inhaled objects, 577
Injections:
intragluteal, 527

Insulin:
  excessive, 342
Insulin levels:
  elevated, 588
Intention, first vs. second:
  healing biopsy, 589
Intercalated disks, 505
Intercostal nerve and vessels, 141
Interleukin-1, 447
Interpeduncular fossa, 27
Intestinal infection, 30
Intestinal loops:
  herniation of, 33
Intravenous drug abuse, 72
Involuntary movements, 442
Ipsilateral hemidiaphragm, 213
Iron:
  excess in liver, 569
Irritants, 1
Ischemia, 358, 364
  myocardial, 602
Ischemic cell injury, 476
Ischiorectal fossa, 436
Isoniazid:
  side effects, 584
Itraconazole, 450
Jaundice, 300, 446
Jejunum, 455
Job's syndrome, 391
Jugular veins, 61
Kallikrein, 60
Kaposi's sarcoma, 64
Kawasaki disease:
  symptoms, 340
Keloids, 136
Keratoderma blennorrhagia, 30
Keratosis:
  multiple seborrheic, 92
Ketoacidosis, 307
Kidney:
  rib fractures and, 362, 400
Kidney disease, 403

Kidney stones, 229
Kidney stones, causes of, 512
Klinefelter's syndrome:
  chromosomal abnormality in, 83
Knee:
  ligaments related to, 66
K-ras mutations, 95
Labia majoris, 33
Labial biopsy, 290
Lamina propria, 98
Langerhans cells, 224
Langerhans' cells, 275
Larvae migrans, 55
Laryngeal nerve, recurrent, 548
  compression of, 266
Laryngeal nerves, 195
Larynx, 464
Latrodecla, 26
Latrodectus mactans, 26
Lead poisoning, 183
Leg fractures, 531
Legionella pneumophila, 572
Leiner's disease, 147
Leprosy, 59, 341
  treatment, 417
Lesch-Nyhan syndrome, 442
Leser-Trélat sign, 92
Leukemia, 481
  acute, 133
  predisposing factors, 96
  child, 86
  chronic, 104
Leukocytes, transmigration of, 21
Leukoplakia, oral hairy, 69
Levator palpabrae superior muscle, 27
Lichen planus, 157, 347
Ligaments, 66, 212, 365, 455, 555, 562
Linear Energy Transfer (LET), 437
Lipoid proteinosis, 117, 430
Liposarcoma, 99, 256

Lips, blue, 402
Listeria, Actinomyces
Liver, 452, 569. See also Hepatic
  cancer
  excess iron, 569
  fatty change in, 20
  hydatid cyst of, 122
LTB4, 60
Lumbar nodes, 6
Lung biopsy, 585
Lung compliance, 372
Lung surgery, 369
Lung tumors, 266
  cancer, 528
  death rate from carcinoma, 43
Lungs, 240, 390, 483, 489
  neutrophil elastase of, 498
Lupus, 101, 354, 465, 594
Luteinizing hormone (LH), 28, 173
Lymph, in thoracic duct:
  lipids in, 129
Lymph nodes, 270, 327, 552
  removal of, 274
  spread of cancer through, 6, 367
Lymph vessels, 327
Lymphatic duct, right, 61
Lymphatic sheaths, periarterial, 565
Lymphatic vessels, 339
Lymphocytes, 20
  neoplasm of, 568
  T-cell, 128
Lymphocytic infiltrate, 243
Lymphokines, 60
Lymphoma:
  Burkitt's, 142, 153
  cutaneous T-cell, 599
Lyon hypothesis, 486
Lyonization, 145
Macroglobulin, 155
Macromolecules, movement into
  bloodstream, 46

Macrophages, 21, 194, 260, 447, 525,
  571, 575
Macular lesions, 30
Malaise, 50
Malaria, treatment of, 211, 465
Male sex characteristics in girls, 160
Mallory-Weiss syndrome, 361
Malnutrition, 592
Marasmus, 592
Marfan's syndrome, 49, 570
Mast cells, 344
  degranulation of, 586
Maxilla fractures, 62
M-cells, 556
Measles, 223
Meat, bacteria from, 506
Mebendazole, 63
Meckel's diverticulum, 71
Mediastinal neoplasms, 114
Mediastinum, posterior, 369
Medium artery, 139
Medulla, 405
Megacolon, 38
Megakaryocytes dysfunction, 162
Meissner's corpuscles, 239
Melanin formation, 360
Melanoma, 235, 274, 420
  biopsy for, 89
  race and, 596
Menarche, age of, 116
Meningioma, 27
Meningitis, 124
  in infants, 371
Menopause, sex hormone levels
  during, 28
Menstrual cycle, 533
Mental disorders, 28, 398, 425, 473
Mesenteric arteries, superior, 152,
  431, 441
Mesotheliomas, 201
Metabolic acidosis, 307
Methemoglobinemia, 402

Methotrexate, 112, 412
Methyl alcohol, 298
MI, acute, 76
Microcephaly, in newborns, 125
Miliaria crystallina, 90
Miliaria ruba, 90
Milkers' nodule, 238
Minoxidil, 495
Mitral valve prolapse, 94
Mohs surgery, 375
Mondor's disease, 312
Mononuclear system, 289
Mononucleosis, 487
Mono-phagocytic system (MPS), 289
Motor function:
  fine, skilled, 204
  voluntary, 204
Mucoid casts, 143
Mucoid medial degeneration, 49
Mucosa, 117, 291
Mucus, cervical, 453
Multiple sclerosis, 165
Muscle disorders, 386
Muscle injury, 140
Muscle strengthening, 501
Muscle tissue, 263
Muscular artery, 139
Muscular dystrophy, Duchenne, 343
Mycobacteria, 59
Mycobacterium leprae, 341
Myconcogenes, 254
Mycosis fungoides, 568, 599
Myeloma, multiple:
  cause of, 185
  diagnostic testing for, 180
Myeloperoxidase deficiency, 225
Myeloproliferative disorders, 135
Myocardial depressant factor, 421
Myocardial infarction, 174, 346, 517, 518
  reperfusion, 602

Myocardial ischemia, 205
Myxoid liposarcoma, 99
Nail bed, reddened, 127
Nails, splinter hemorrhages on, 271
Nasal cavity, 291
Nasal concha, 291
Nasal congestion, 232
Nasal mucosa infection, 81
Neck tumors, 213
Neck wounds, 464
Necrobiosis lipoidica diabeticorum, 591
Necrolysis, toxic epidermal, 215, 262
Necrolytic migratory erythema, tumors associated with, 521
Necrosis, 200, 202
  immune-mediated vascular damage and, 78
Neisseria meningitidis, 337
Neoplasms. See Cancer; Tumors
Nephrotoxicity, 434
Nerve regeneration, 447
Neural tube defects, 82
Neuroblastoma, 254
Neurofibrillary tangles, 32
Neurofibromatosis, 19
Neuropathy, peripheral, 282
Neutrophil elastase (NE), 498
Neutrophils, 21
Nevi, 420
Niacin deficiency, 253
Night blindness, 123
Nonpolyposis, hereditary, 24
Obligate aerobe bacteria, 59
Obligate anaerobes, 8
Obturator internus muscle, 18
Ochronosis, 110
Oculomotor (CN III), 27
Oligodendrocytes, 165
Onchocerciasis, 379
Oncogenes, 95, 254

Onycholysis, 118
Onychomycosis, 450
Opsonization, 168
Oral contraceptives, 116, 346
Organisms, types of, 432
Organophosphate overdoses, 56,
  119
Orthostatic hypotension,
  assessment of, 444
Osler's nodes, 514
Osler-Weber-Rendu disease, 322
Osmolality, 426
Osseus neoplasms, 224
Osteitis deformans, 163
Osteitis fibrosa cystica, 210
Osteoclasts, 33, 210
Osteoporosis, fractures and, 496
Osteoprogenitor cells, 244
Ototoxicity, 434
Ototoxicity, 11
Ovarian arteries, 365
Ovarian cancer, 367, 529, 601
Ovaries, 472
Ovulation, 453
Oxybutynin, 4
Oxygen-hemoglobin dissociation
  curve, 13
P53 mutations, 95
Paget's disease, 163
Paint chip ingestion, 183
Palindromic sequence, 257
Pancreas, 421, 431
  uncinate process of, 441
Pancreatic insufficiency, 206
Pancreatic tissue in small intestine,
  87
Pancreatic tumors, 588
pain referred from, 422
Pancreatitis, 471
Panic in public places, 398
Panniculitis, histocytic cytophagic,
  236

Papilloma virus, 560
Paraesthesiae, 10
Paraprotein, 416
Parasites, 106, 508
Parasitosis, delusions of, 497
Parathyroid gland, 7, 278
  removal of, 3, 32
  tumors of, 272
Parathyroid hormone, 32, 272
Parotid gland cancer, 351
Patent ductus arteriosus, 439
PDGF-beta subunit, 105
Peanuts, carcinogen associated
  with, 316
Pedal edema, 516
Peligra, 253
Pelvic cavity, 515
Pelvic splanchnic nerves, 314
Pelvis, tumors of, 2
Pemphigus vulgaris, 353, 355
Penicillin class antibiotics, 167, 287
Perimysium, 263
Perineal space, 463
Perineum, anesthetizing the, 68
Peritoneal cavity, 5
Peritoneum, 455
Periumbilical pain, 172
Peroneal nerve, 545, 597
Peroneal vessels, leg fractures and,
  531
Petechiae, 72
Petit mal, 460
Peutz-Jeghers syndrome, 74
Peyer's patches, 424
  surface epithelium covering, 556
PH, hydroxide ion concentration
  and, 47
Phagocytic cells, 225, 289
Phenylalanine, 313, 454
Phenylketonuria, 454
Phenytoin, side effects, 107
Pheochromocytoma, 42

Philadelphia chromosome, 481
Phobias, 398
Pimozide treatment, 188
Pinocytotic vesicles, 247
Piperazine, 63
Pituitary fossa, 23, 583
Pituitary gland, 88
  veins from, 445
Placental barrier, antibodies that
    cross, 261
Plasma cells, 21
Platelets, 94, 162, 542
  deficiency of, 162
Plexus, choroid:
  tumor in, 480
Pneumococcus, 232
Pneumonia, 176, 488, 572
  eosinophilia, 143
Poisoning, 119, 127, 150, 183, 368
Polyarteritis, in children, 75
Polyarteritis nodosa, 166
Polychondritis, 299
Polycythemia vera, 135
Polyps, 74, 95
Pox virus, 238
Preaortic nodes, 6
Pregnancy:
  age of first, 116
  complications of, 530
  cutaneous eruption during, 484
Procainamide, 382, 594
Processus vaginalis, 33
Progesterone levels:
  drops in, 31
  in menopause, 28
Propantheline, 4
Prostaglandins, 60
Prostate cancer, 255, 267
Prostate gland, inferior surface of,
    137
Protamine, 598
Protease inhibitor, 155

Protein deficiency, 592
Protein fibrils, 332
Proteins, 82, 117, 309, 416, 471
  Factor VIII, 269
Prothrombin time, elevated, 218
Prothrombotic vs. antithrombotic
    factors, 108
Proto-oncogenes, 95
Protozoa, 432
Pruritic erythematous papules, 65
Pseudotumor cerebri, 563
Psoriasis, 30, 118, 465
  treatment, 113, 419
Psoriatic arthritis, 419
Ptosis, 27
Pubic rami fractures, 542
Pudendal canal, 18
Pudendal nerve, 68
Pulmonary embolus, 542
Pulmonary infarction, 346
Pulmonary infections, 206
Pulmonary vascular congestion, 525
Pulmonary vessels, 489, 544
Pupillary light reflex, 27
Purine base, 115
Purkinje fibers in heart, 523
Pustules, on distal extremities and
    face, 65
Pyknosis, 476
Pyloro-duodenal junction, 25
Pyoderma gangrenosum, 134
Pyrantel pamoate, 63
Pyrimidine, 115
Quinidine, side effects of, 93
Rabies virus, 475
Radiation, 171, 437
  cell resistance to, 39
  used to treat mycoses fungoides,
    599
Radiosensitivity, 34
Rashes, 215
Rectal bleeding, 551

Rectal fistula, surgery to drain, 436
Rectosigmoid region, 38
Rectouterine pouch of Douglas, 51
Red blood cell antigens, 44
Red blood cells:
    abnormal, 393
    destruction of, 194
    excessive production of, 135
Reed-Sternberg cells, 396, 554
Reiter's syndrome, 30
Renal artery, 279
Renal failure, 12, 198
    edema and, 40
Renal stones, causes of, 512
Replication error phenotype, 24
RER+, 24
Respiratory distress, 213
    in infants, 292, 319, 429
Respiratory system, 138
Reticulated erythema, 53
Reticulated hypopigmented
    pattern, 53
Retinopathy, in children, 75
Retroviruses, 170, 264
Reye's syndrome, causes in
    children, 329
Reynaud's phenomenon, 333
Rhabdovirus, 475
Rheumatic fever, 399, 580
Rheumatoid arthritis, 100
Rhodopsin synthesis, 123
Rh-positivity, 507
Rib fractures, 362, 400
Rickets, 9
Rickettsia, 248
Rifampin, 538
RNA, 474
Rocky Mountain spotted fever, 477
Rogaine, 495
Romana's sign, 259
"Rose spots," 144
Rubella eruption, 179

Salicylate toxicity, symptoms of, 303
Salmonella infection, 144
Saphenous vein, 457
Sarcoidosis, 138
Sarcoma. See also Liposarcoma
    Kaposi's, 249
Scalene muscle, anterior:
    tumor on, 385
Scalp, 182
Scar tissue, 136
Scarpa's fascia, 311
Schilling test, 567
Sclerosing cholangitis, primary, 296
Scrotum, 33
Scrotum cancer, 491
Scurvy, 447
Sebaceous gland, 370
Sebum, 370
Secretions, antibodies in, 219
Seizures, 216, 460
Self-mutilation, 442
Sella turcica, 23
Septic shock, 488
Sexual intercourse:
    anal, 148
    painful, 102
Shock, 294, 488
    stages of, 394
Shunting procedures for
    hypertension, operative risk
    for patients undergoing, 587
Sickle-cell disease, 393
Sinusitis, chronic:
    treatment, 232
Sjögren's syndrome:
    diagnostic tests for, 290
    manifestations of, 377
Skeletal muscle fibers, 140
Skin, flushing of, 524
Skin diseases, 215. See also
    Dermatological symptoms
    cancer, 235, 242

melanoma, 89, 235, 274, 420, 596
  treatment, 375
Skin lesions, 136, 235, 239
  macular vs. papular, 101
  vascular, 249
Skin pigmentation, 103
  bluish-black, 110
SLE, manifestations of, 354
Smoke inhalation, 127
Smoking, 227
Sodium nitrate, 368
Spastic movements, 442
Sphenoid bone, 23
Sphenoid sinus, 583
Sphincter muscles, drugs that relax
  the, 4
Spina bifida, 82
Spinal nerves, dorsal roots of, 10
Spinal tumors, 10
Spine, 110, 204, 480
Spleen, 194, 565
Splinter hemorrhages, 72
Spondylitis, ankylosing, 30
Staphylococcal abscesses, "cold," 391
Staphylococcus aureus, 72, 193, 469
Staphylococcus ssp, 22
Stasis, 108
Sternum injuries, 159
Steroid hormones, 217
Steroid-producing cells, 131
Steroids, topical, 301
Stethoscope, 478
Stomach, tears in, 361
Streptococcus, 41, 469, 488
  Group A, 399
Streptococcus ssp, 449
Strokes:
  detection, 94
  embolic, 94, 174
  treatment, 174
Subclavian vein, 61
Submental nodes, 29

Submucosal glands of Brunner, 25
Superoxide dismutase, organisms
  lacking, 389
Surfactant deficiency, 429
Surgical incisions, muscle fiber
  direction and, 89
Surgical procedures, antibiotic
  prophylaxis for, 72
Sweat duct obstruction, within
  stratum corneum, 90
Swimming pool granulomas, 59
Syncopal attacks, 444
Syndrome X, 181
Syphilis, 191
Systemic lupus erythematosus
  (SLE), 101, 354
Takayasu's arteritis, 227
Tapeworms, 122
Tendons, 241, 513
Tensor fascia latae muscles, 17
Testes, undescended, 558
Testicular cancer, 558
  lymphogenous spread of, 6
Testosterone/estradiol ratio, in
  menopause, 28
Tetany, 3
Tetracycline, side effects in
  children, 48
Theca interna, secretion of, 111
T-helper cells, 568
Therosclerotic lesions of arteries,
  331
Thiabendazole, 63
Thoracic duct, 252, 369
Thoracolumbar fascia, 311
Thrombi formation, 108
Thromboangiitis obliterans, 227
Thrombocytopenia, 284
Thromboembolism, 158
Thrombolytic therapy, 518
Thrombophlebitis, 45, 312
Thrombosis, 85, 166, 384, 446

deep venous, 346
Thymic corpuscles, 58
Thymomas, 114
Thymus, children born without, 234
Thyroid gland:
  destruction of C-cells in, 541
  isthmus of, 175
  surgery, 32, 352
  thyroidectomy, 3, 7, 32, 130, 195, 548
  underactive, 522
  vessels of, 130, 252, 278, 352
Thyroid tumors, retrosternal, 114
Tibial artery, anterior, 597
Tinea versicolor, 308
T-lymphocytes, 97, 234
Tonsils, palatine, 492
Toxic epidermal necrolysis (TEN), 215, 262
Toxic shock syndrome, 193
Tracheal anatomy, 226
Tracheitis, 226
Transesophageal echocardiogram, 94
Transfusions, complications of, 468, 534
Transplant organ rejection, 97
Transversalis fascia, 494
Trazodone, side effects of, 574
Trichinosis, 271
Triglycerides, 129
Trisomy, 133, 380
TRNA, 553
Trousseau, 45
Trypanosoma cruzi, 67, 259
Trypanosomiasis, American, 67, 259
Tryptophan, 459
Tuberculosis, 59, 200, 538
  drug treatment, 584
Tumoral calcinosis, 12
Tumors, 2, 10, 266, 385, 403, 420, 480, 485, 520, 521, 563. See

also Cancer
  with anterior mediastinum mass, 114
  brain, 42, 160, 440, 520
  chromosomes and, 559
  differential diagnosis of specific types of, 42
  gastric, 482, 577
  G-cells, 577
  hepatic, 213, 266, 346, 459, 521
  Pancoast, 240
  pancreatic, 422, 528, 588
  pseudotumor cerebri, 563
  soft tissue, 209
  thyroid, 114, 272
Typhus, etiology of, 248
Tyrosine, 360, 454
Ultravate, Topical, 301
Umbilical arteries, 2
Umbilical ligament, median, 212
Uncinate process, 431
Urachus, 212
Uracil, 474
Urbach-Weithe disease, 117
Ureter nerves, 229
Urethral sphincter, loss of control of, 493
Urethritis, nongonococcal, 30
Urinalysis, 110
Urinary bladder, 314, 543
  cancer of, 285, 552
  training, 4
Urine, 463
  orange, 246
Urogenital atrophy, 28
Urogenital diaphragm, 137, 463
Urticaria, 122
Uterine artery, 515
  thrombosis of, 85
Uterine cycle, 504
Uterine tube, 151
Uterus, 102, 408

Vaginal fornix, posterior, 51
Vaginal lubrication, 98
Vagus nerve, 338, 577
Valves, heart, 94, 399
Varicella zoster, 35
Vascular disease, 166
Vasculitis, 166
Vaughn Williams classes, 120
Veins, 61, 339
    microanatomy of, 357
Vena cava, inferior, 279
Venereal warts, 560
Vertebrae, radiodensity of, 110
Vessels, 139. See also specific
    vessels
Virchow's triad, 108
Viruses, 35, 170, 238, 475, 560. See
    also Epstein-Barr virus
    classes of, 264
    types of, 35
Vitamin A, 573
    deficiency, 123, 581
Vitamin B12 absorption, 443, 567
Vitamin B1 (thiamin) deficiency,
    154, 282
Vitamin C deficiency, 447
Vitamin D, 217
    deficiency disorders, 9

excessive, 512
Vitamin K, 196
Waardnburg-Klein syndrome, 366
Walendstrom's macroglobulinemia,
    418
Warfarin, 411, 427
Waterhouse-Friderichsen
    syndrome, 337
Watershed infarcts, 294
Wegener's granulomatosis, 227
Werner's syndrome, 532
Wernicke-Korsakoff syndrome, 154
White forelock, 366
Wickham's striae, 157
Wilms' tumor, 403
Wilson's disease, 37
Winkler's disease, 378
Wiskott-Aldrich syndrome, 284
Woods lamp, 192
Woronoff ring, 315
Wrinkles, 89
X chromosomes. See
    Chromosomes, X
Xeroderma pigmentosum, 242
Yersinia enterocolitica, symptoms
    of, 50
Zane platelets, 542
Zinc deficiency, 470